Cake
DECORATING

Cake DECORATING

FAY GARDNER

CASSELL

I dedicate this book to my wonderful husband Ken, who has never said, 'not cake decorating again', to my three treasures John, Pam and Joanne who have always shown great interest, and to the Good Lord who always guides my hands.

A CASSELL BOOK

First published in the United Kingdom 1993 by
Cassell
Villiers House
41/47 Strand
London WC2N 5JE

First published in Australia in 1988
by Angus&Robertson Publishers
Published by arrangement with Bacragas Pty Ltd
This second edition published in Australia by Angus&Robertson,
an imprint of HarperCollins*Publishers*
25 Ryde Road, Pymble, Sydney NSW 2073, Australia

British Library Cataloguing-in-Publication Data:
A catalogue record for this book is available from the British Library.
ISBN 0 304 34356 0

Cakes on pages iii and contents page decorated by
Margaret Rogers and Dianne Kunzli.
Cover photograph Quentin Bacon.

Printed in Hong Kong

Contents

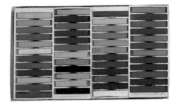

Introduction

The idea for a book on cake decorating has been in my thoughts for many years. I have tried to bring you my experiences of over 35 years of decorating and teaching; to pass on my ideas and methods.

For the beginners I have included step-by-step photographs and instructions. If you follow them closely they will help you over any problems you may encounter. I hope the advanced decorator will feel the freedom to experiment based upon the ideas in the book and that the blending of my ideas with yours will lead to some exciting work.

I have covered flower making in the book in three sections, starting with the simplest flowers and progressing to the more advanced flowers. Hopefully the chapter on wildflowers will bring some interesting variations to your decorating. There are also chapters on ornaments, marzipan, chocolate and, of course, cake making and royal icing.

As I planned the outline of the book I was reminded of the many wonderful years of pleasure cake decorating has given me and the treasured friends I have made. I hope you, too, will have as many hours of creative enjoyment and pleasure.

EQUIPMENT KEY
(See photograph opposite)

1. Nylon brushes
2. Non-toxic chalks
3. Ruler
4. Spatula
5. Pastry brush
6. Rolling pins
7. Cutting board
8. Stemtex
9. Ribbon
10. Cornflour (US cornstarch)
11. Drying stand
12. Pure alcohol and colour
13. Non-toxic chalk dust
14. Wire
15. Shaping block
16. Level
17. Liquid colours
18. Petal dust
19. Non-toxic pens
20. Oval cutters
21. Patty tins
22. Jaconette and Jaconette bags
23. Tubes
24. Cutters
25. Toothpicks
26. Modelling and shaping tools
27. Teflon cutting board
28. Pillars
29. Pallets
30. Brushes
31. Moulds
32. Knives and scalpels
33. Emery boards
34. Grater
35. Leather tools
36. Crimpers
37. Stamens
38. Leaf-veiners
39. Scissors
40. Dried Baby's breath
41. Tube brush

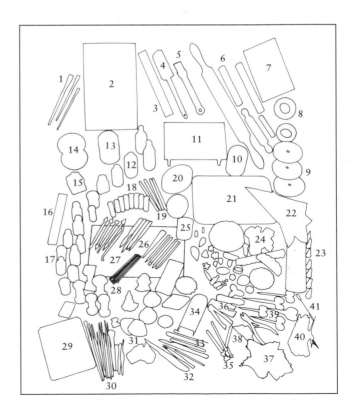

Part I
PREPARATION

Equipment

Equipment and supplies for cake decorating can be obtained from either most health food stores or specialised cake decorating supply stores.

Icing Bags

Jaconette, a material which is rubberised on one side, makes the best icing bags. Unlike nylon or plastic, it does not allow the heat of your hands to penetrate it and affect the consistency of the icing.

Care of the bag is simple. Just wash in cold water, turn inside out and hang up to dry. As soon as the rubber starts to perish, discard the bag. Once the bag becomes permeable, the egg white in the icing may seep through it, spoiling the consistency of the royal icing.

You can buy bags ready-made from any health food store or make them yourself. The material is available from most large stores. One-quarter of a metre (¼ yard) of jaconette will make four 23 cm (9 in) bags. Cut the material into four squares. Using one square, fold the material diagonally, rubber-side inwards, bringing C up to B (see diagram below). Use a sewing machine to stitch from A to B twice, close to the edge. Make sure that the machine needle is sharp. A blunt one will make large holes and the icing could seep through them.

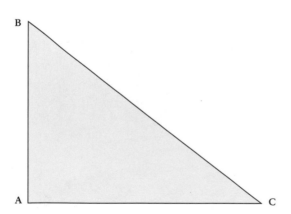

Paper Icing Bags

If you have to use a number of different coloured icings, a disposable paper icing bag is the answer.

Cut a square of greaseproof paper diagonally to make a triangle. Make a tight cone with a closed point along the straight edge, following pictures 3 to 6. Fold the top edge in and over, following

pictures 8 to 10. Secure the edge with adhesive tape to maintain the shape. Cut a small hole in the point

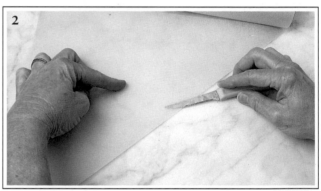

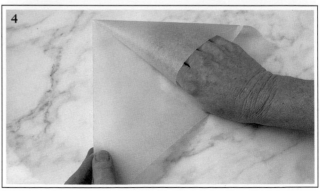

of the cone. Insert the chosen piping tube and make any necessary adjustments. Never fill the bag more than half full.

These bags can also be used without a tube by cutting a small hole in the point of the cone. For leaf design, cut away each side to form an inverted 'V'.

Screws or Adaptors

These are inserted into a jaconette or nylon bag so that the icing tubes can be changed without having to empty the bag. When a bag wears out, remove the screw and use in a new bag.

To insert the screw, turn the bag inside out and push its point up as far as possible. Place the screw

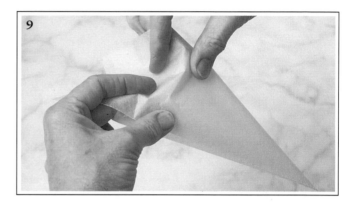

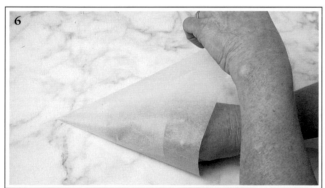

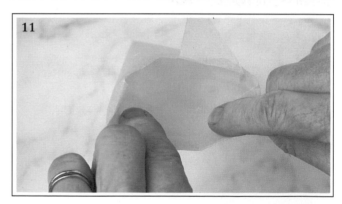

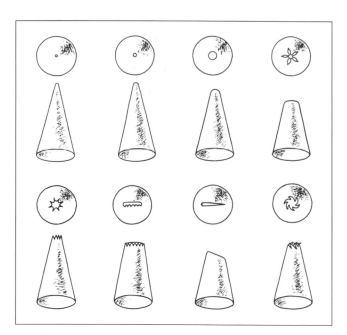

upside down on the end of your finger and push right up into the point of the bag. Keep the point of the bag in the centre of the round part of the screw. If it is off-centre, you will have problems when the icing tube is screwed on. Take a long double thread of strong cotton and, leaving a tail for tying, wind the cotton securely around the furrow part of the screw. Tie off the cotton neatly. Turn the bag right-side out and make sure the end of the screw is protruding from the point of the bag. Turn the bag inside out again, and cut and trim the bag around the edge of the screw base.

Tubes and Pipes

There are many different types of tubes and pipes used for piping royal icing. They are screwed onto the screw or adaptor. Some of the tubes and pipes available include:
• writing tubes, which have plain round holes and come in sizes 00–4

• stars, serrated and claw-like, sizes 5–15
• petal or rose, left-handed or right-handed, sizes 20, small, medium and large
• basket weave, sizes 22 and 23
• leaf, sizes 16 and 17
• half-shell, sizes 35, small, medium and large.
   A basic kit would consist of sizes 00, 0, 1, 2, 8, 12, 16, 22 and 35.

Icing (Confectioner's, Powdered) Sugar

Always use pure icing (confectioner's, powdered) sugar. Never use icing mixture. It contains cornflour (US cornstarch), which will prevent the royal icing reaching the right consistency.

Mixing Bowls

All bowls used for mixing icing should be made from glass or ceramic. Metal will discolour the icing. Plastic is too soft and can give when the icing is being mixed, affecting its consistency.

Cake Tins (Pans)

Cake tins (pans) are available in aluminium or heavy galvanised tin. These days they come in many different shapes — eg, hearts, diamonds, blossoms, fans, as well as the more usual round, square and oblong shapes. Shop around for a good selection.

Patty Tins (Pans)

These are used to hold the moulded flowers while they are drying, so it is worthwhile buying a clean, new set. The shallow tins (pans) found in supermarkets are good enough.

Rolling Pins

You can use plastic, non-stick or wooden rolling pins for modelling. An ordinary kitchen rolling pin will do for covering a cake with almond paste, but for covering with fondant you will need a pin approximately 46 cm (18 in) long (not including the handles). I prefer a turned wooden one.

Waxed Paper

The cheap varieties available from the supermarkets can be used. The waxy surface allows icing to be set or piped onto it and, when dry, can be peeled off. Greaseproof paper is not waxy enough to use for this purpose.

Greaseproof Paper

A cheap variety will do, providing it is strong, as it is used mainly for lining cake tins (pans) and making paper icing bags.

Brown Paper

Brown paper is used for lining cake tins (pans). The brown paper sold in rolls for covering schoolbooks is cheap and is free of creases.

Cake-board Paper

Use good-quality silver or gold paper specially made for covering cake boards. Other types of paper may tear and mark. Never use aluminium foil to cover a cake board. It creases and tears, lowering the standard of the decoration.

Florist Tape

There are two types of florist tape, Stemtex and Parafilm. I prefer Stemtex, and use it very sparingly. It is used to join wired icing flowers together in a spray.

Work Board

Glazed tiles, a heavy sheet of glass or a wooden board all make a good, non-stick work board for modelling and cutting out modelling paste.

Cake Boards

Use strong masonite that is at least 3 mm (⅛ in) in thickness. If it is any lighter, the weight of the cake could cause it to bend. This may damage the cake decoration.

Cornflour (US Cornstarch)

Use Wade's cornflour (US cornstarch) to dust your hands when modelling paste. Any other brand is too gritty. Potato flour is also very good.

Scissors

The small pair of scissors used when making flowers are the most important ones. They must leave your fingers easily when you wish to put them down, and they need to have a long, narrow cutting edge. You will need a pair of kitchen scissors for cutting paper. Wire scissors or pliers are also a must.

Scalpel, Probe and Long-nose Tweezers

These are essential for many areas of cake decorating and can be bought from cake decorating suppliers.

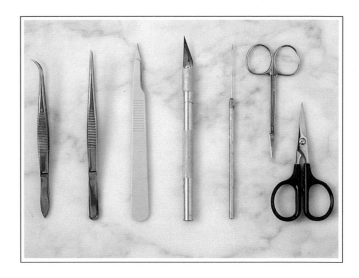

Flower Cutters

The latest way of making flowers for cake decoration is to use flower cutters. There are many different types on the market. However, I think it's important to learn to make the flowers freehand before beginning to use cutters, so that this more creative approach to cake decorating survives.

Flower Shapers

Tools of different shapes and sizes are needed for hollowing out the paste cone to make a flower shape. I use round toothpicks (wooden picks), hair-roller pins, golf tees and bought, wooden or plastic shapes. The ball tool is used for cupping petals. The dog-bone tool is used for fluting the edges of petals.

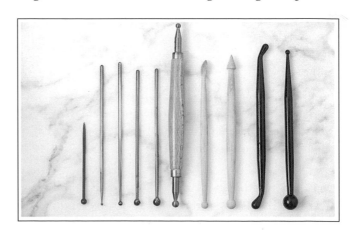

Moulds

Moulds of many different sizes and shapes are available on the market for moulding cake ornaments.

Formers

A former is coned-shaped and used to form the throat of a flower during moulding. It is available in various sizes and is made of plastic or wood.

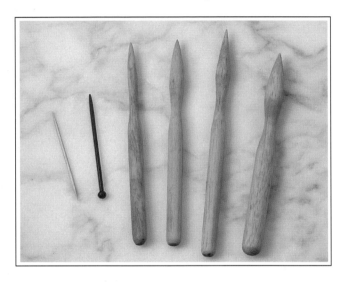

Icing Floats

These are flat pieces of board, at least 27½ cm (11½ in) long, with a cutting edge. They are used for smoothing the almond paste or fondant over the cake. I use an icing float that I purchased or 2 pieces of flat, unblemished board. A plain, plastic tumbler is a good substitute when smoothing a round cake.

Spirit Level

A miniature spirit level will take the guesswork out of applying almond paste or fondant evenly.

Drying Racks

A wooden drying rack allows the wire stem of a completed flower to pass through it and the flower to nestle in the concavity. You can buy perspex ones for drying small flowers. If neither is available, you can use polystyrene foam.

Stamens

There are 3 kinds on the market, round heads, half heads and very fine heads. All have their uses, and you can choose the ones you prefer to fill the centre of your flowers. Once you have used the head of a stamen, the thread can be used by itself. Threads coloured with a darker colour look very natural.

Icing Colourings

Always use the best quality food colourings available. Poor-quality colours do not contain a stabiliser and will separate and spot the fondants. Always shake the bottle well before use and use sparingly. I like the bottles of liquid food colouring that have an eye-dropper (most British brands).

Pure Alcohol

Pure alcohol is used to mix the colour that is applied to flowers made from white modelling paste or icing. Pure alcohol can be hard to obtain, so I suggest you use a clear spirit eg, vodka, cooking vodka, gin etc.

Colouring Chalks

These must be the special, non-toxic alpha pastels. They are either grated or rubbed onto cartridge paper to form a fine dust, which is then applied to a modelled or piped flower with a nylon brush.

Petal Dusts

These were created in Britain as a substitute for the dust from grated, non-toxic chalks. They meet the very strict requirements of the British health laws, so are safe to use.

Paintbrushes

It is worth spending a little extra to collect a selection of top-quality brushes in different sizes. They make cake decorating much easier.

Wire

For many years I have used Australian rayon-covered wire for wiring flowers. You can buy fine, medium or heavy wire. A British paper-covered wire is good for heavier headed flowers.

Ribbon

Ribbon is readily available, in widths ranging from very narrow to wide. Keep different widths and colours on hand.

Cake Making

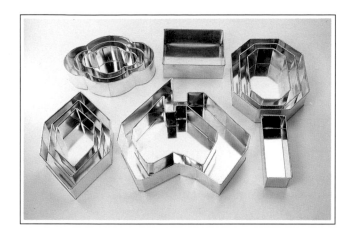

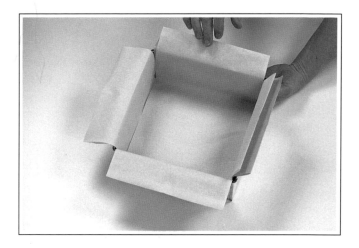

LINING THE CAKE TIN (PAN)

Before you start to make the cake, line the tin (pan). Keep the linings simple and easy to handle. I have found the following methods best.

To Line a Square Tin (Pan)

Cut 4 sheets of brown paper and 4 sheets of greaseproof paper. They should be as wide as the inside of the tin (pan) from one side to the other. The length should be equal to the inside width of the tin, plus the height of the 2 sides, plus 5 cm (2 in).

Place 2 sheets of brown paper, one on top of the other, into the tin, leaving about 2½ cm (1 in) of paper above the rim of the tin; take them down one side of the tin, across the bottom and up the other

side, creasing them at the bends. You should have 2½ cm (1 in) of paper protruding above the opposite rim to where you started. Turn the tin 90° (a quarter-turn) and repeat the process using the other 2 sheets of brown paper. The tin should now be completely covered. Repeat this with the grease-proof paper.

This method allows the lining to be peeled away without damaging the cooked cake. It is very important that the cake is as perfectly shaped as possible.

To Line a Round, Heart-shaped, Six-sided, Eight-sided or Oval Tin (Pan)

Cut a double thickness of brown paper that is the height of the tin (pan) plus 2½ cm (1 in) and the length of the circumference of the tin. Do the same with greaseproof paper.

Tape the 4 sheets together using sticky tape so that they can be picked up as one unit. This lining goes inside the tin.

Position it so that the bottom edge just touches the base of the tin. Now press it against the sides of the tin around the entire shape, creasing it into any corners if necessary. Make sure it is held in position by taping the paper to the outside of the tin.

Now cut 2 sheets of brown and 2 sheets of greaseproof paper in the shape of the base of the tin, and carefully insert them.

The tin is now fully lined. The sticky tape will probably leave marks on the tin, but this method makes a perfectly shaped lining.

At one time, if you wanted a cake to be a particular shape, you had to cook it in a conventional tin, then cut it into the shape required. This wasted a lot of cake. Now you can get tins in all sorts of imaginative shapes and different sizes.

Tins made of galvanised, heavy-duty tin cook cakes more quickly than aluminium tins do. I counteract this by tying newspaper (3 sheets thick) around the outside circumference of the tin. The tin

can then be buttered and floured, or sprayed, instead of being lined. This method is very useful if you are dealing with tricky shapes.

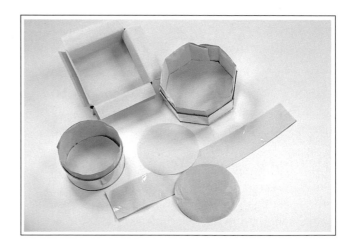

FRUIT CAKE

Fruit cake has plenty of body and will tolerate the handling that occurs when it is being covered with almond paste and fondant. Try my recipe — it is basic but has proved to be very popular.

Let's talk briefly about ingredients. I prefer butter to margarine; caster (superfine) sugar to brown (soft, light) sugar, and overproof rum or brandy to sweet sherry. I always use large eggs to make sure their combined weight equals that of the butter. I use plain (all-purpose) flour, and seldom use self-raising flour. Parisian essence, in moderation, is better for giving colour than bicarbonate of soda (baking soda), which only just darkens the mixture.

Good-quality, mixed dried fruit, bought from the supermarket, is as suitable as the one you would mix yourself. The quality of the fruit is very important. Raisins should be plump and big enough to be cut into four pieces. Sultanas (golden raisins) should be a 5-crown grade at least; they keep the cake moist. Currants should never be less than 4-crown grade; if they are smaller, they will cook in the first hour in the oven and become dry, giving the cake a burnt taste. Always use real glacé (candied) cherries, not the imitation ones made from turnip; they cook into hard lumps. It is essential to use diced, not sliced, mixed (candied) peel.

These days all good-quality dried fruit is washed before it leaves the drying sheds, but if you insist on washing the mixture again, make sure it is thoroughly dry before you use it. Wet fruit sinks to the bottom of the cake. Our grandmothers always soaked the fruit in rum or brandy for weeks before they made the cake. It certainly does wonders for the flavour, but there could be a soaked piece of fruit near the top of the cake which you may be unlucky enough to pierce while covering the cake with fondant, and you would get an unattractive brown mark on the fondant. I never take the risk.

This recipe is for a 21 cm (8½ in) square cake tin (pan) or a 23 cm (9 in) round cake tin. It can be doubled for a 26 cm (10½ in) square tin or halved for a 15 cm (6 in) square tin.

Recipe

250 g (8 oz) butter
1¼ cups (250 g, 8 oz) caster (superfine) sugar
1 tablespoon vanilla essence (extract)
5 large eggs
3 tablespoons overproof rum
3 cup (360 g, 12½ oz) plain (all-purpose) flour, sifted
1 tablespoon Parisian essence
1¼ kg (2½ lb) mixed fruit
1 tablespoon golden syrup (light treacle)

Method

Cream the butter and sugar until light and fluffy. Place in a large mixing bowl and add the vanilla essence. Beat the eggs, one at a time, with an electric mixer and add to the creamed mixture (batter), beating well after each addition. Add rum and stir through the mixture. Gradually add the sifted flour, blending it in until evenly distributed. Add Parisian essence and stir in. Lastly, add the mixed fruit and golden syrup and mix well. The mixture is now ready to be spooned into the tin (pan).

Preheat the oven to 150°C (300°F). While the oven is heating, spoon the cake mixture into the lined tin. Don't just scoop it into the middle; pack it into the sides and corners, using all the mixture. Level the top of the mixture with a wooden spoon. Pick up the tin and drop it gently on the table. This will eliminate air bubbles and allow the cake to keep level as it cooks. It is important to keep it as level as possible, for you will later turn it upside down to cover it with almond paste and fondant.

Reduce the oven heat to 140°C (275°F). Place the cake in the oven so that the top of the tin, not the paper protruding from the top of the tin, is approximately in the middle of the oven. Only do this when the required temperature has been reached. Do not open the oven door for the next 2½ hours.

To test if the cake is done, insert a pointed steak knife into the middle. Do not use a straw or a metal skewer. They are too thin to give a correct reading. The wide surface of a knife is more accurate. If the knife comes out clean, the cake is done; if it doesn't, put the cake back in the oven and cook for a little longer. Listen to your cake to see if it is done. Cakes

'sing' while they are cooking, the singing stops when they are done.

When you are satisfied that the cake is done, wrap it without delay, still in the tin, in a clean towel and leave until it has completely cooled. This will take about 12 hours. On no account attempt to take the cake out of the tin until you are sure there is no heat at all left in the cake.

LIGHT FRUIT CAKE

Recipe

250 g (8 oz) butter
1¼ cups (250 g, 8 oz) caster (superfine) sugar
4 eggs
2 cups (250 g, 8 oz) plain (all-purpose) flour
½ cup (60 g, 2 oz) self-raising flour
½ teaspoon salt
1 teaspoon mixed spice (Pumpkin Pie Spice)
1¼ kg (2½ lb) mixed fruit
½ cup (60 g, 2 oz) almonds, chopped
3 tablespoons rum, sherry or brandy

Method

Cream butter and sugar together. Add the eggs, one at a time, beating well after each addition. Sift together the flours, salt and mixed spice. Stir in the dry ingredients alternately with the mixed fruit and almonds. Lastly, add the rum and mix well.

Spoon the mixture (batter) into a lined 21 cm (8½ in) cake tin (pan). Bake in a slow oven for about 3½ hours. (Refer to the instructions for your own oven to determine what temperature is recommended for a 'slow oven'. This can vary according to the make and type of oven.)

PROBLEMS

If your cake is less than perfect, you will probably have made a mistake with timing or temperature.
1 ✻ If the cake is dry and crusty on the top, the oven was too hot.
2 ✻ If the top is split, the oven was too hot. Fortunately you can remedy this. As soon as you take the cake from the oven, place an upturned saucer over the cake and wrap the cake, still in the tin, in a clean towel and leave until it is completely cool. When you unwrap it you should find that the crack has closed up.
3 ✻ If the cake is too dry, it has been cooked too long.
4 ✻ If the cake has a wet spot in the middle of the bottom, it hasn't been cooked long enough. Fruit cakes cook slowly from the edges and the middle is the last part to cook.

SPONGE CAKE

Recipe

3 eggs
½ cup (135 g, 4 ½ oz) caster (superfine) sugar
1 cup (120 g, 4 oz) self-raising flour
1 tablespoon butter, melted
3 tablespoons hot water

Method

Grease two 17½ cm (7 in) sandwich tins (layer cake pans) and flour lightly. Set oven temperature at 170°C (350°F). Separate the eggs and beat the whites until they are stiff. Add sugar gradually, beating until mixture (batter) is thick, then add the beaten yolks. Sift the flour and fold into mixture lightly and evenly. Add the melted butter and the hot water quickly and stir in. Mix thoroughly.

Pour equal amounts of mixture into the 2 tins and bake in the moderate oven for approximately 20 minutes. Turn out onto a wire rack to cool. Spread chosen filling on 1 cake and place the other one on top.

BASIC BUTTER CAKE — MADEIRA

This is the recipe to use when making cream-covered novelty cakes for children. Bake it in a 27½ x 17½ cm (11 x 7 in) lamington tin (jelly roll pan). From a cake slab of this size, you will have plenty of cake to cut out all the shapes you need. A packet cake mix also gives good results.

Recipe

120 g (4 oz) butter
½ cup (135 g, 4 ½ oz) caster (superfine) sugar
1 teaspoon vanilla essence
2 eggs
2 cups (250 g, 8 oz) self-raising flour
½ cup (120 ml, 4 fl oz) milk

Method

Grease sides and line the bottom of the lamington tin. Set oven temperature at 150°C (350°F). Cream butter and sugar until white and fluffy. Add vanilla essence. Gradually beat in the lightly beaten eggs. Sift flour a couple of times. Fold into the creamed mixture (batter) alternately with the milk, starting and finishing with the flour. When the mixture is smooth, pour into the tin and bake 20–25 minutes. When cooked, cool on a wire rack before cutting.

Covering the Cake

ALMOND PASTE

In my opinion, the almond paste is as important as the final fondant covering, for it allows you to mend any imperfections in the shape of the cake.

Until the Second World War, almond meal was always used to make the paste, but when almonds became scarce, marzipan meal was used instead. Almond meal is blanched, ground almonds. Marzipan meal is the ground inner kernels of stone fruit such as peaches and nectarines. Apricot kernels are no longer used because they have been found to contain cyanide. I like marzipan meal. It smells, tastes and works just like almond meal, but because it is less oily, it has the added advantage that it does not bleed through the fondant and leave ugly blotches, which almond meal has been known to do.

Before you start to make the paste, assemble your equipment. You will need a clean working surface, a pastry brush, a rolling pin, a spirit level, and 2 light, flat pieces of board or an icing float for levelling and flattening.

Recipe

1¼ cups (120 g, 4 oz) almond or marzipan meal
3 cups (500 g, 1 lb) icing (confectioner's, powdered)
  sugar
1 egg yolk
1 medium lemon, squeezed
sweet sherry, same amount as lemon juice
1 teaspoon glycerine
egg white for glazing (see p 14)

Method

Mix meal and icing sugar together in bowl. In another bowl beat the egg yolk into the lemon juice and the sweet sherry. Add the glycerine and stir well. Add the liquid to the dry ingredients slowly, mixing as you go. Continue mixing until the dough leaves the sides of the bowl cleanly.

Sprinkle a little icing sugar on the pastry board or workbench. Put the dough on the board and roll out. If it sticks to the board, add a little more meal or icing sugar. If it is crumbly, add a little more liquid. When it rolls out smoothly, you are ready to begin covering the cake.

Note

The cake must be as perfectly shaped as possible. Take it out of the tin (pan), turn it upside down and see if it sits flat on the board. Since cakes do not always rise completely evenly, it probably will not sit flat. Turn the cake on its side and, with a very sharp knife, cut down a little way along the edge of what will be the base of the cake; turn the cake slightly and make another cut level with the first one. Continue turning and cutting the base in this way until you have cut right through. The cake should now be level enough to sit flat on the board. Do not, on any account, cut straight through from one side to the other. It's almost impossible to get the base even in this way. Instead, you will possibly find that what began as a ½ cm (¼ in) cut on one side ends up being a 2½ cm (1 in) cut on the other.

COVERING THE CAKE

1 ✠ From the rolled-out paste, cut a strip as wide as the height of the cake, and as long as the measurement from the middle of one side of the cake, around the corner to the middle of the adjoining side. Never put paste on from corner to corner; it must always go around the corners.

2 ✠ Glaze one side of the paste with egg white.

3 ✠ Starting at the middle of one side of the cake, place the glazed side of the strip against the cake and neaten it in place with either the two flat boards or the icing float.

4 ✠ Repeat steps 1 to 3 for each side of the cake. Make the joins as undetectable as possible.

5 ✤ Now you have to cover the top. To get the exact shape, place the cake tin (pan), rim down, on the rolled-out paste and trace around it with a sharp knife, making the cut as neat as possible.

6 ✤ To smooth the paste covering, roll the rolling pin gently up one side of the cake, over the top and down the opposite side. Repeat on the other sides.

7 ✤ When you are satisfied with the smoothness of the paste covering, glaze it with egg white. This will seal it.

8 ✤ Put a piece of waxed paper on a spare piece of board, place the cake on it and cover. Leave to dry for at least 24 hours.

9 ✤ If you are unfortunate enough to find the paste is uneven once it has dried, use some extra paste, glazed on one side with egg white, to make the covering level.

Glaze the top of the cake with egg white.
Do not glaze the paste. Lift the cut paste carefully and place it on the cake so that it fits against the top edge of the side pieces of paste. Gently pinch the edges of the top and sides together and smooth so that no join is apparent.

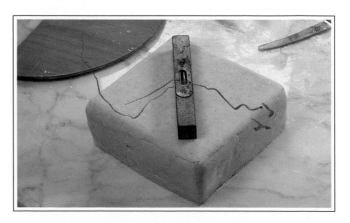

Note
When you are attaching the paste to the cake, use just enough egg white to make the paste sticky. If you use too much, the paste will 'float' and cause the final covering of fondant to move and separate.

FONDANT

Fondant is the final coating of the cake and therefore must be free of all marks, air bubbles and cracks. The process of applying this final coating is called 'covering'.

Below are 3 recipes. The first, for super-fondant, is the one I always use. The second is a quicker one, very handy if you are icing only 1 cake. The third has a creamy look and is therefore better for coloured fondants than a white one.

There are a few things to bear in mind when covering:
1 ✳ Do not do it in the heat of the day.
2 ✳ Do not do it when you are tired. Covering can be hard work, and if you are weary the result is likely to be poor.
3 ✳ If you wish to colour fondant, always do it in natural light, never under artificial light.
4 ✳ Make absolutely certain that your hands and workbench are spotlessly clean.
5 ✳ Warn the family. Once you have started covering, nothing must be allowed to interrupt you.
6 ✳ Don't wear a dark, fluffy jumper or anything made of material that will 'fleck'. You could find some unwanted bits in the fondant.

Recipe 1 — Super-fondant

The ingredients fall into 3 groups:

GROUP 1
2 cups (500 g, 1 lb) white granulated sugar
⅓ cup (120 g, 4 oz) liquid glucose
2 tablespoons glycerine
1 level teaspoon cream of tartar
⅔ cup (150 ml, 5 fl oz) water

GROUP 2
2 tablespoons gelatin
⅔ cup (150 ml, 5 fl oz) water

GROUP 3
120 g (4 oz) copha (white vegetable cooking fat, (white) shortening)
1½ kg (3½ lb) icing (confectioner's, powdered) sugar

Method

Grease the inside rim of a 2 litre (3½ UK pint, 4¼ US pint) saucepan to a depth of 2½ cm (1 in). Put the first 5 ingredients (group 1) into the saucepan and stir continuously over a medium heat until all ingredients have dissolved and the liquid is starting to boil. Reduce heat, but keep the mixture boiling until it reaches a 'soft ball' consistency (110°C (240°F)). Turn the heat off.

Put the gelatin and water (group 2) into a second saucepan and stir over a medium heat until the gelatin has dissolved. On no account allow the liquid to boil or you will create an imbalance in the mixture (but do make sure the gelatin is dissolved). Turn off the heat.

Add dissolved gelatin to the contents of the first saucepan, taking care that there is no overflow. Cut the copha into pieces and add to the mixture. Let it stand until the copha has dissolved. Put the mixture in a heatproof mixing bowl. It is now ready to be mixed. There are two methods for doing this:
1 ✳ Add the icing sugar gradually to the liquid mixture, stirring well between each addition. Cover the bowl when everything is well mixed and leave to stand for 24 hours.
2 ✳ Put the icing sugar into the heavy-duty bowl of an electric mixer. Add the hot liquid and mix on speed 2 for 2 minutes. Do not allow the mixer to labour. When the mixture is smooth, cover the bowl and leave to stand for 24 hours.

Immediately before you begin to cover the cake, you will need to knead more icing sugar into the fondant. Take a small piece and knead icing sugar into it until it becomes soft.

Repeat this process for the entire mixture. Now knead all the fondant together until it is white, firm and not sticky. If it can hold its own weight when it is held up and squeezed in the middle, it is the right consistency.

Recipe 2

1 tablespoon (15 g, ½ oz) gelatin
¼ cup (60 ml, 2 fl oz) water
½ cup (120 ml, 4 fl oz) liquid glucose
1½ tablespoons (23 ml, ¾ oz) glycerine
30 g (1 oz) copha (white vegetable cooking fat, (white) shortening)
1 kg (2¼ lb) icing (confectioner's, powdered) sugar

Method

Sieve icing sugar into a bowl. Put gelatin and water in a saucepan, and thoroughly dissolve over a medium heat. Do not allow it to boil. Add glucose and glycerine to hot liquid and stir until combined. Add copha, allow to dissolve. Stir liquid into icing sugar, which has been sieved. Knead in the bowl until combined, then remove and knead on workbench (counter) until smooth and pliable.

Colour if desired. The fondant is now ready to roll out and apply to your cake.

Recipe 3

3 cups (500 g, 1 lb) icing (confectioner's, powdered) sugar
1 egg white, unbeaten
¼ cup (60 ml, 2 fl oz) liquid glucose

Method

Sift the icing sugar into a bowl and make a well in the centre. Add egg white and warmed glucose and blend until the mixture can be handled. Take out of the bowl and knead into a pliable paste, which can now be rolled out and put on the cake.

COVERING A CAKE WITH SUPER-FONDANT

Make the required amount of fondant. To give you an idea of the amount of fondant you will need, a 21 cm (8½ in) square cake will take one-third of a batch made using the quantities shown in the recipe. Keep covered once it is made. Glaze the cake with egg white so that the almond paste is sticky but not sloppy. Put the cake to one side. Cover a cake board (see p 26), and place a small piece of waxed paper in the middle.

Sprinkle sifted icing (confectioner's, powdered) sugar on the workbench (counter). Place the ball of fondant on the icing sugar and knead icing sugar into it, carrying out the procedure described on p 16. Continue until the fondant has become firm, white and not at all sticky. By the time it has reached the correct consistency, the original ball will have nearly doubled in size. If you intend to have coloured fondant, add the colouring about two-thirds of the way through the kneading process.

When you are satisfied with the consistency of the fondant, put the ball in a bowl, cover it and leave for an hour. While you are waiting, tidy the workbench and bring the cake which is to be covered to your work area. Place your icing floats or pieces of flat board within easy reach. You are now ready to begin covering the cake.

1 ✻ Dust the workbench with icing sugar. Dust your hands lightly also.

2 ✻ Dust a 46 cm (18½ in) rolling pin with icing sugar.

3 ✻ Roll the ball of fondant in icing sugar on the bench and re-knead it gently.

4 ✻ Roll the fondant out. To prevent the centre sticking to the board, and to get an even thickness, roll the fondant then turn it a few degrees, roll and turn again. Continue doing this until you have an evenly flat sheet of fondant. Do not make the sheet too thin as any unevenness in the almond paste will show through.

5 ✻ Prick any air bubbles and gently roll again.

6 ✻ Pick up the sheet of fondant by draping it over

the rolling pin in the same way you pick up a sheet of pastry.

Place it against the back side of the cake, bring it up over the top and down the front side.

The cake should be completely covered. Consult the photographs if you are in any doubt.

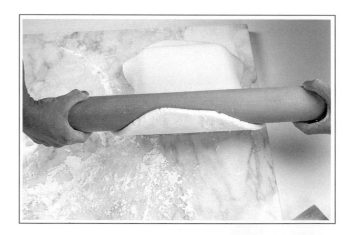

7 ✻ Take a flat board dusted with icing sugar and gently press the fondant down on the top of the cake.

Do it carefully, as you must get rid of any air bubbles that may be trapped under the fondant. With the cupped palms of your hands, ease in the corners so that the fondant fits the cake and gently rub them. Make sure your hands are not sticky.

Dust them with more icing sugar if necessary.
8 ✳ Using the icing floats or flat boards, cut off any excess fondant around the bottom of the cake.
Do it straight away. If you delay, the weight of the excess fondant will pull down the fondant covering the shoulder of the cake. This will result in cracking.

9 ✳ Neaten the bottom edge very carefully.
10 ✳ Straighten, smooth and polish the covering, using the boards, until you feel it is perfect.

11 ✳ Place the covered cake on the specially covered cake board. It is now ready to be decorated.
The procedure for covering a cake is the same if you are using the fondants from recipes 2 and 3.

Note
When handling the fondant, make sure your hands are cool and not sticky. Keep them lightly dusted with icing sugar.

Cake Boards
A badly covered cake board will detract from the appearance of a decorated cake, so time spent on this part of the process is never wasted.

Single-tier or bottom-tier boards must have cleats on the underside, both to strengthen the board and to allow your fingers to fit under the edge during

lifting. You can use either two strips of beading or a smaller board of the same shape. The cleats on boards used for show cakes must either be covered

in the same paper as the board or painted to match.

The covering paper can be glued to the board with thick white paste, thin white paste, thin white glue or wallpaper glue. Make sure the glue is evenly distributed so that no lumps show through and it won't loosen around the edges. Silver and gold paper look very attractive. Aluminium foil is not a suitable cover. It creases and is not strong enough.

To Cover a Square, Six-sided, Eight-sided or Corner-cut Board

Cut a piece of covering paper 5 cm (2 in) larger than the board and place the paper, wrong-side up, on the table. Apply paste over the entire surface of the smooth side of the board and place it on the

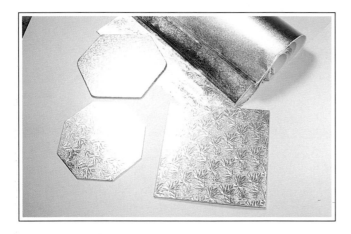

paper, leaving a 5 cm (2 in) border of paper around the edge. Turn the board and paper over and smooth the paper down with a soft rag.

Turn the board over again. Now fold the paper border back so that it can be pasted to the underside of the board. The corners should be neatly mitred and there should be no bumps along the edges. Mitring is not difficult; most of us will remember being taught how to do it when we covered our school books. Work slowly.

Carefully paste the paper border along one side of the board, then turn it over and press it down evenly to the underside of the board. Do the same with the opposite side. Mitre each of the 4 edges in turn. Crease the paper well and keep it as flat as possible. Paste the remaining 2 borders and press down onto the underside of the board. Make sure that all the layers of paper are firmly stuck.

To Cover a Round, Oval, Heart-shaped, Blossom-shaped or Any Round-edged Board

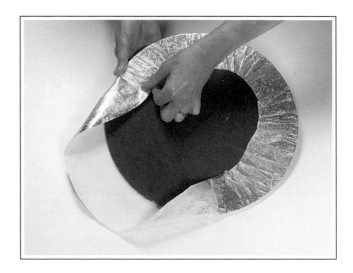

Cut the covering paper in the same shape as the board, allowing an additional 6 cm (2½ in) margin all around. Place the paper, wrong-side up, on the workbench (counter). Paste the smooth side of the board and lower it onto the paper, centring it and leaving a border protruding equally around the board. Turn the board back over and smooth the paper down with a soft rag, making sure there are no lumps. Paste the border paper and, gathering it in to fit as you go, press it down onto the underside of the board. Make sure it is neat and flat.

Part II
DECORATING

Royal Icing

PREPARING THE ICING

Royal icing is used for all piping work. The batch must keep its shine and elasticity while being made, so follow the instructions carefully. Otherwise, the icing will be heavy and dull, and the thread of icing will not flow easily through the piping tube.

Recipe

1 unbeaten egg white
icing (confectioner's, powdered) sugar, sifted

Method

1 ✳ Place the egg white, which must be used at room temperature and must be free of any yolk and thread, into a clean glass or crockery bowl.
2 ✳ Add sifted icing sugar, 2 teaspoons at a time, and beat with a wooden spoon between additions. Continue doing this until the mixture forms neat peaks.
3 ✳ Cover the bowl at once, otherwise a crust will form on the icing. If a crust does form, do not attempt to beat it into the batch. Throw it away. No matter how hard you beat, it will not blend with the rest of the icing. Remove any icing residue from around the bowl so that the crusts cannot fall into the mixture.
4 ✳ If you have to leave the icing to stand for any length of time before you are ready to fill your icing bag and start work, beat the icing before you put it into the bag. The egg white quickly settles to the bottom, so make certain that it is blended in and the icing has the correct overall consistency.

If you want to colour royal icing, use liquid food colouring. Compensate for the additional liquid in the colouring by using a little more icing sugar.

ROYAL ICING CONSISTENCY

1 ✳ Small peak consistency: for general piping of dots, lines, writing, lattice, scallops, the royal icing should hold its shape when pulled to a small peak between the finger and thumb.
2 ✳ Petal consistency: for star work with serrated tubes, and for making flowers with petals that must stand up, the royal icing must be stiffer. Add 2 more spoonfuls of icing sugar to the small peak consistency mixture. The peak of royal icing on the back of the spoon should hold its shape when the spoon is lifted from the bowl.
3 ✳ Soft peak consistency: is a little looser than the small peak consistency mixture and is used for embroidery, lace and extension work.

PROBLEMS

1 ✳ If the mixture is too soft, add more icing sugar.
2 ✳ If it is too heavy, add just a touch of egg white to bring it back to the right consistency.
3 ✳ If it is dull and heavy, you have added too much icing sugar too quickly and have not beaten the mixture well enough between additions.
4 ✳ Never use icing mixture. This has cornflour (US cornstarch) in it and will give you the incorrect consistency.
5 ✳ I don't believe you should keep royal icing in the refrigerator: the covered bowl can form condensation and the recipe does not call for water.

LEARNING HOW TO USE ICING BAG AND TUBES

You have to learn how to hold the bag, how to apply pressure so that the icing will emerge from the tube's nozzle steadily and not in fits and starts, how to make straight lines, both upwards and downwards, how to make loops, dots and lattices, how to write names and numbers. You also have to familiarise yourself with different types of tubes and the icing consistency needed for them. Only practice will enable you to do all this, so don't feel it's a waste of icing and time if all you do for a while is make practice patterns on a plain masonite board. It is important to gain perfect control. Some people manage this more quickly than others, but as long as you get there, why worry? Patience always pays off.

To fill a bag with royal icing, fit the chosen tube onto the bag and turn the top half of the bag over the outside.

Lay the bag across your hand and spoon in the royal icing.

Turn the top half of the bag back up and squeeze the icing down into the bag. Twist the top half of the bag around.

It is best to begin with a writing tube. They come in sizes 00, 0, 1, 2, 3 and 4. Start with the largest one you have. Attach it to the adaptor on the bag. Fill the bag with royal icing and fold the top over as instructed. Place the bag across your open hand with the folded top just under the thumb muscle.

Close your 4 fingers around the bag and keep your thumb on the folded top.

The pressure to force the icing through the tube must come from your 4 fingers, not from the thumb. Squeeze the bag and a thread of icing will emerge; stop the pressure and the thread will not come out.

Hold the bag with your elbow lifted and the nozzle of the tube pointing downwards. Squeeze the bag gently and as the thread begins to emerge, guide it in the direction you wish it to go. Using a large writing tube, practise making straight lines first, then add some loops and dots.

When you begin to feel confident, move on to the star and petal tubes and the fine writing tubes. For writing and embroidery, hold the bag at a 45° angle. For stars and dots, hold it at a 90° angle.

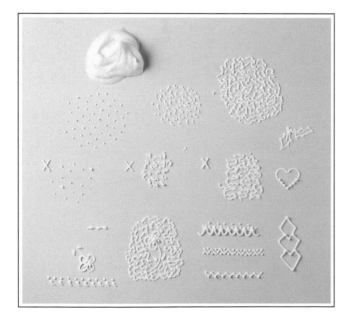

EDGINGS

If you find the icing is beginning to blob and the stars are indistinctly marked, the icing has become too soft. You will have to take it out of the bag and beat it again, possibly adding a little more icing sugar.

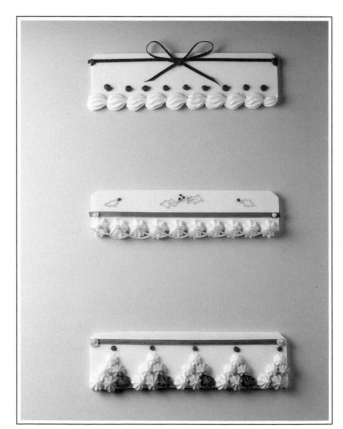

Edgings, or borders as some people call them, are very important to the look of the finished cake. When you come to make them, you will see how essential it is that the bottom edges of the cake are neat and the coverings of almond paste and fondant icing are smooth, level and as exact as possible.

Borders around the bottom edges of a cake are piped with royal icing. The simplest edging is the shell pattern. The icing must be stiff enough (petal consistency) for the shell shape to be clearly defined. If the icing is too soft, the edges of the design will 'blur'. The shells must be of equal shape and size, and should overlap, the top of each shell pattern taking in the tail of the preceding one. You can be as imaginative as you like when designing borders and making patterns using the different tubes. The plain writing tube can be very handy here.

LACE

This is made on creased waxed paper. Fold the sheet of paper in half, then crease it in parallel lines approximately 1¼ cm (½ in) apart. Do not concertina the paper; it must lie flat on the workbench (counter). Creased wax paper is used because it allows the icing to dry quickly and to be picked up easily when the lace pattern is complete.

Lace is made using loops, dots, scrolls etc. It is important to work slowly and carefully, and to make sure that each stroke joins.

Fill the icing bag with royal icing of soft peak consistency and screw a size 00 writing tube onto the adaptor. Hold the bag at a 45° angle. Pipe slowly, pressing the bag all the time. You should be able to just feel the paper under the tube end. Lace is piped downwards from the straight edge formed by the crease in the waxed paper. This allows the loops to flow in a more natural curve than if you were working in the opposite direction, taking them upwards. Make sure that each stroke joins the previous stroke so that the finished lace can be picked up in one piece.

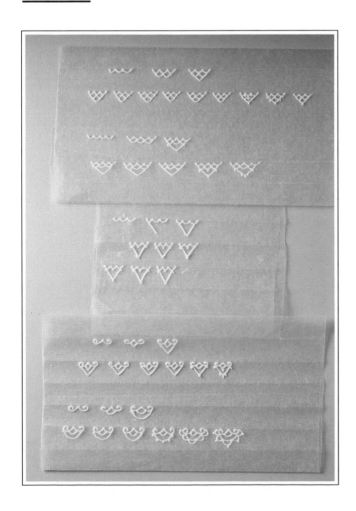

You do not have to pipe a long straight edge to make a top border for the lace piece. Such a border would make the completed lace bulky and hard to handle when being attached to the wet joining thread that is used to attach it to the cake. When you pipe your first row, make sure that no icing protrudes above the crease in the paper. Also make sure that you keep the paper straight. Otherwise, the finished lace will be at a slant and you won't be able to use it.

EMBROIDERY

Designs for finely piped embroidery for the top and sides of a cake can be copied from material, lace, baby clothes, tablecloths and embroidery transfers. As you become more proficient, you will even be able to use the design of the bride's dress as your pattern, or be able to follow the floral theme of the bridal bouquet. Dainty animal patterns suitable for christening cakes will also become easy.

You can build up the design, stroke by stroke, if you feel confident enough. However, if working freehand is too daunting, trace your chosen design onto greaseproof paper and retrace onto the fondant of the cake using a knitting needle. It seems hardly necessary to say — go carefully.

Use a size 00 writing tube and royal icing that is at a soft peak consistency. Some people prefer to

use a paper cone instead of an icing bag; they hold it as they would a pencil.

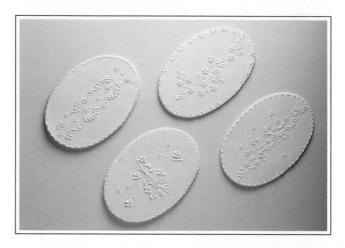

The first exercises should involve making loops, lines, dots, stems, leaves, teardrops and simple flowers such as the forget-me-not. Using a light touch, feel the fondant under the tube as you work. If the designs run and start to look messy, the icing is too soft. You will have to thicken it with a little more icing sugar and start again.

BRUSH EMBROIDERY

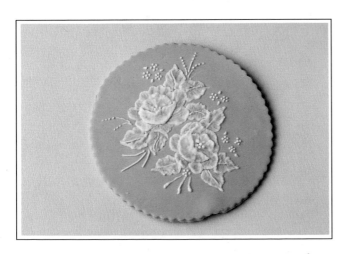

This is an icing technique created to resemble the embroidery that is used on tablecloths, placemats etc where satin stitch is used to fill in the petals and leaves of the design. It can be reproduced in icing quite quickly and easily, highlighting and shading with colour to give a very soft and delicate result.

Transferring the Design
Three different methods can be used.

Method 1 — Transferring with Perspex
I prefer this method because it avoids the possibility of pencil smudges marring your work. The icing embroidery must be ready to use before the cake is covered.

1 ✳ Using either a piece of perspex or glass (remember to tape the edges to avoid cutting into the fondant) place the design underneath the perspex or glass and outline it with royal icing using either a size 00 or size 1 tube. Allow this to dry thoroughly.

2 ✳ Press the royal icing design into the soft fondant to leave an impression. Remember this method gives a mirror image but the design can be reversed before it is piped onto the perspex. It gives a very clear outline for you to follow.

Method 2 — Transferring with Pencil
1 ✳ Outline the design onto tracing paper and then reverse the paper and outline the underside, using a non-toxic pencil.

2 ✳ Using an empty ball-point pen trace through the design onto the fondant to give you a clear outline.

Method 3 — Pin Pricking
This method would only be suitable for small areas, as it can become very confusing once you start to cover some of it with royal icing.

Method 4 — Knitting Needle Transfer

1 ✳ With a pencil, outline the design onto grease-proof paper leaving out the fine details. Keep the pencil lines as light as possible.

2 ✳ Place the paper onto the cake, secure with a pin and carefully scribe through with a knitting needle that has a blunt end.

Starting the Design

If you are a slow worker, add 1 teaspoon of piping gel to every 4 tablespoons of royal icing (this must be freshly made and of a piping consistency). I also find it very helpful to have a small amount of piping gel near as I work. I wipe the brush onto it and then into the royal icing as I begin to work down the petals. Do not use a lot of gel at any one time because it has a yellowish colour and could mar your work.

1 ✳ Start at the back petals and outline once, then place the second outline inside the first, working on only a small section each time.

2 ✳ With a dampened (not wet) size 2 or 3 sable mix brush (a good-quality brush is important to achieve an even finish) work the two outlines

together and down to the end of the petal, filling as you go and fading towards a thin film of the icing as you reach the pointed end of the petal.

Try to create the effect of satin stitch embroidery, which is heavier at the rounded end of the petal and thinner towards the pointed end.

3 ✳ When thoroughly dry, pipe in details such as stems, stamens, veins etc.

4 ✳ Next colour in highlights and shadows with food colour diluted with a spirit (vodka, pure alcohol etc) rather than water, to avoid wetting the work.

The colour contrasts you can achieve with this technique are beautiful. Brown on pale apricot — red on white — white on any colour background. It also works very well as a background to moulded flowers placed as a spray within the brush embroidery area.

BLUEBIRDS AND DOVES

These little birds can perch on the top or the side of a cake. Doves are made of plain white royal icing, bluebirds from royal icing that has been coloured a pale baby-blue. Make an entire bluebird from the same batch of icing, otherwise you could get a two-tone bird.

Making the Birds

You will need a batch of royal icing, a sheet of waxed paper and an icing bag fitted with a size 00 tube.

Fold the waxed paper in half, then crease it in parallel lines approximately 1½ cm (½ in) apart. Do not concertina the paper. It must lie flat on your working surface. Add 2 teaspoons of sifted icing sugar to the royal icing you have made, which should be of a small peak consistency. You need the extra stiffness so that you can give the tail and wings of the bird a genuinely feathered look. Put the icing in the bag.

The Tail

The tail is made up of 3 feathers, a long one in the centre and a shorter one on either side. Begin with the outside left feather. Starting at the crease in the waxed paper, pipe at a 45° angle to the left, and without stopping the flow of icing, come back to your starting point. Now pipe the middle feather. Pipe from the crease straight up and back again, making this feather longer than the first one. Come to the crease again and pipe the right feather at a 45° angle to match the left one. All this should be done in one continuous flow. (See the photographs opposite.)

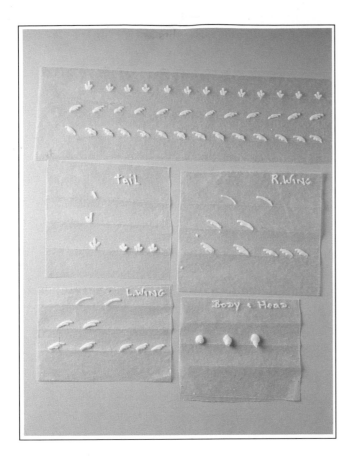

Right Wing

Using a continuous thread of royal icing and working to the right, make 3 slightly overlapping lines of diminishing length. These should curve slightly, and must finish at the same starting point.

Left Wing

Follow the procedure for the right wing, but work in the opposite direction.

Place the wings and tails to one side and allow to dry thoroughly.

Body

Keeping the piping tube at an angle, squeeze out a body shape. Release the pressure and move the tube slightly forward, pipe a little head and pull up quickly so that the icing forms a beak. The head should, of course, be attached to the body. (See the photographs above.) Do not forget to make a spot of colour for the eyes.

Assembly

While the body is still wet, attached the dry tail. Carefully place the dry wings on either side of the body, just below the head. You know the shape of a bird — follow it as closely as you can.

Note

Two birds on any one cake are sufficient.

Modelling Pastes and General Techniques

MODELLING PASTES

Most of the ornaments used to decorate cakes are made from pastes that are variations of a type of gum paste Greeks used for their confectionery many generations ago. I use 2 different recipes.

Recipe 1

This is excellent for fine work, but a batch must be used up once the extra icing sugar has been added. Remember that it doubles in quantity with the additional sugar, so only make the amount you need.

2 tablespoons (20 ml, 1 fl oz) water
2 level teaspoons gelatin
1 rounded teaspoon liquid glucose
⅔ cup (150 g, 5 oz) icing (confectioner's, powdered) sugar

Method

Heat the water and gelatin in a small saucepan over a medium heat. Stir with a teaspoon until the gelatin is completely dissolved. Do not allow the mixture to boil or else the liquid balance of the recipe will be lost.

Turn off the heat. Using the hot teaspoon, take up a rounded spoonful of liquid glucose and stir it into the mixture. Pour mixture into a clean bowl. Add the icing sugar, a spoonful at a time. Beat in well after each addition. When the mixture is smooth, cover the bowl and leave it for 8 hours.

Recipe 2

This recipe includes gum tragacanth. The recipe does not require the addition of more icing sugar once it is made, and I like it for this reason. However, because it has a higher fat content than Recipe 1, it is harder to colour.

3 cups (500 g, 1 lb) icing (confectioner's, powdered) sugar
1 level teaspoon gum tragacanth
3 level teaspoons gelatin
3½ tablespoons (50 ml, 1½ fl oz) water
3 level teaspoons liquid glucose
2 level teaspoons copha (white vegetable cooking fat, (white) shortening)

OPPOSITE: Violet

Method

Place the icing sugar and gum tragacanth in a crockery or glass bowl. Mix together with a wooden spoon. Dissolve the gelatin in the water in a small saucepan over medium heat. Make sure the liquid does not boil. Take the saucepan away from the heat. Add the liquid glucose and the copha to the dissolved gelatin. Stir with a wooden spoon until the mixture is smooth.

Pour slowly into the icing sugar mixture and mix until the resultant paste is stiff enough to handle. Take paste out of the bowl. Knead on a board lightly covered with icing sugar until all ingredients are well combined. Put the ball of paste into a plastic bag and place in a sealed container. Leave for 48 hours. The paste will then be ready to use.

PROBLEMS

1 ✳ If the paste is greyish, you did not follow the instructions and either used a metal spoon or a metal container. A wooden spoon and a glass or crockery bowl must be used at all times.
2 ✳ If the paste is heavy and rubbery, with no pull in it, you have added too much gelatin.

Note

Measurement of the ingredients in these 2 recipes must be precise, otherwise the consistency of the paste will be wrong and you will find it very difficult to use.

GENERAL TECHNIQUES

Bean and Cone Shapes

These are the basic shapes from which most small flowers are made.
1 ✳ Roll paste into a 3 mm (⅛ in) ball.
2 ✳ Form the ball into a cone shape by rolling it lengthways, shaping a point at one end and a rounded top at the other.
3 ✳ Using a toothpick (wooden pick) hollow out the cone ready to make a flower.

Long and Short Cuts

The size of a petal is determined by the length of the cuts made in the rim of the cone of paste. A short cut of 3 mm (⅛ in) deep is suitable for a stubby petal. A long cut, to make a longish petal, would be 6 mm (¼ in) deep.

Five Equal Cuts

Cut the first petal to size, then cut a petal of equal size on either side of it. Make the last cut to halve the remaining piece.

Mending Petals

Whether you cut the paste with a knife, cutter or scissors, the edges will always look a little torn. Gently smooth them between your thumb and index finger to give a natural look.

Petal Thickness

When you hollow out a cone of paste to make a flower shape, the thickness of the petals will be determined by how thin you make the paste around the upper rim.

Mitring

This is the term used for cutting a petal into shape. A long mitre makes a pointed petal. A short mitre makes a snub-nosed petal. A round mitre makes a gently rounded petal.

Fluting

There are 3 methods of fluting:
1 ✳ Place the moulded petal on a flat board and gently run a dog-bone tool around the petal edges.
2 ✳ Place the moulded petal on a flat board. Place a round toothpick (wooden pick) so that a small part of its length lies on the petal and the rest is on the board. Roll it gently to and fro, pressing on the part of the toothpick that is on the board, not the other part.
3 ✳ This is the method I use most. Take the upper edge of the moulded petal between the thumb and forefinger. Push the finger forward and pull the thumb backwards at the same time. Practise on

thick paste to begin with. As you get the feel of it, use thinner and thinner paste. Once you have mastered the technique, you will be able to vary the fluting.

Wiring

A wire with a hooked end is used for wiring most flowers and all buds. The exception is a bell-shaped flower. Knot the wire, leaving the length needed below the knot. Cut the wire closely above the knot. It can now be drawn through and buried in the bell of the flower without spoiling its shape. To wire a large flower such as a daffodil, make a wired calyx in the appropriate size, dampen it and attach it to the base of the dried flower.

Drying

Some articles need to be made from a block of paste (eg, baby booties, animals, books etc). Always pierce holes in the underside of the block of paste so that it can dry from the inside easily. If left to dry from the outside only, a gas forms in the wet inside of the block. This will either split the block open or crack it badly.

Arranging

No 1 size flowers are the large ones which make the focal point of a spray (eg, frangipanis, roses, daisies).

No 2 size flowers are smaller flowers used to accompany the main flowers. They can also be made up into a spray for a smaller cake by using 6 or more wired together with buds (eg, japonica, mint ladies).

No 3 size flowers are called 'filler flowers'. They come in several sizes. Groups of 3 tiny flowers and a bud will fill the very smallest spots. Three flowers, about 1 cm (½ in) in size, wired together with a bud, can be used to fill the area around larger flowers, softening and padding out the whole spray.

Flower Centres

Always use plenty of stamens. Wherever possible, I prefer to remove the stamen heads and use only the threads. I paint the tips a dark colour, which gives a very natural look. Never let the royal icing that holds the stamens in place be visible when the flower is finished. If the flower has a domed centre (eg, carnations, sweetheart roses), take particular care in the way you fit the inner petals together.

Buds

Buds can be:
• short and bulbous
• short and pointed
• long and thin.
The shape of the flower will indicate the shape of the bud.

1 ✵ Place a ball of modelling paste over the hooked end of a piece of wire. Quickly attach the bottom of the paste to the wire while it is still damp enough inside to grip the wire. Now shape the top end into the desired bud.

2 ✵ Paint a tiny calyx in very pale green at the bottom of the bud. Do not make the colour heavy. Too much green in a delicate flower arrangement can be overpowering, particularly in a design for a wedding cake. Paint the top of the bud to match the flower's colour. Some buds can be entirely green, as if they have not yet begun to open.

Leaves

You can use special cutters to make leaves, but they are simple to mould freehand. The best way is to press a real leaf onto wet paste — this gives you shape, veining and imprint, all in one go. If using the freehand method, cut out the leaf and mark the veins to make them look as natural as possible. If the leaf has a serrated edge, make the tiny cuts with the well-sharpened end of a small, narrow knife. The cuts must be clean. Never leave a leaf flat. In their natural state, they all have slight curves of one sort or another.

Leaf colouring is very important. If the scheme of your design is darker colours, the natural colour of the leaves will look right. But if the flowers are pale, dark green leaves could be overpowering. Use your discretion, both for the depth of colouring and the number of leaves.

Flower Making for Beginners

DAINTY BESS

The shape of this flower comes from the dog rose, which has 5 petals, as long as they are wide, and a centre filled with stamens. I take the heads off bought stamens and tip the stalks or threads with a darker colour, giving the flower a more natural look.

Note
The scissors, knife or cutters used to cut out the petals will tear the edges slightly. Mend the edges by patting them gently between thumb and forefinger, making them look soft and natural.

ABOVE: *Ballerina Rose*

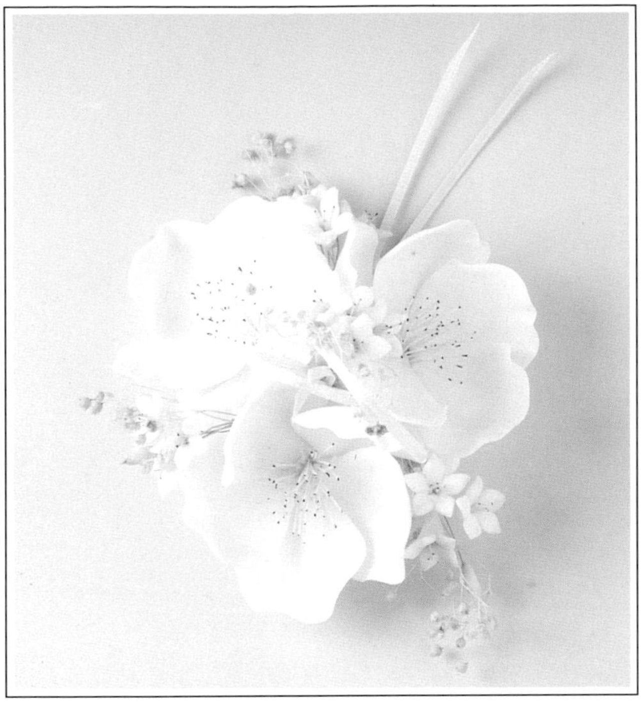

Making the Petal

1 ❋ Take a ball of white or coloured modelling paste, about 1 cm (½ in) in size, and gently roll into a bean shape.

2 ❋ Keeping a point at one end and a smooth top at the other, flatten and widen the bean by gently patting it between the thumb and forefinger of both hands. Make the rounded, top edge as neat as possible using your fingers.

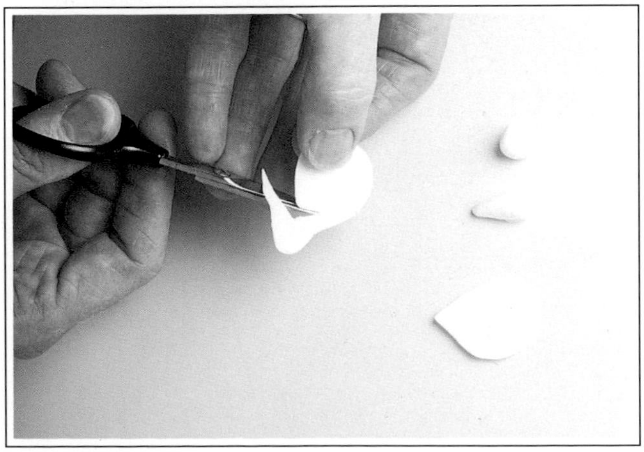

3 ❋ If the petal has become longer than it is wide, cut it into shape, starting halfway down one side and finishing halfway up the other. Do not cut the rounded, top edge, because you could lose the shape.

Shaping the Petal

You can do this in 4 different ways:

1 ❋ Place the petal in the centre of the palm of your left hand. Keeping that hand loose, press the thumb or forefinger of your right hand into the paste so that it forms a cup shape. Do not close the left hand over the petal.

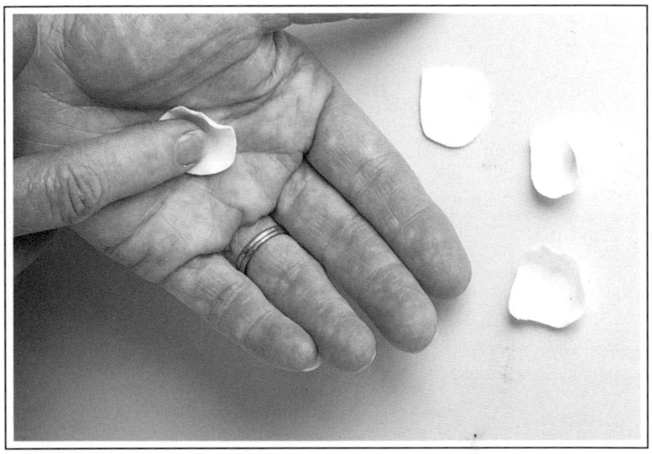

2 ❋ Gently press a dog-bone tool around the outer edge of the petal.

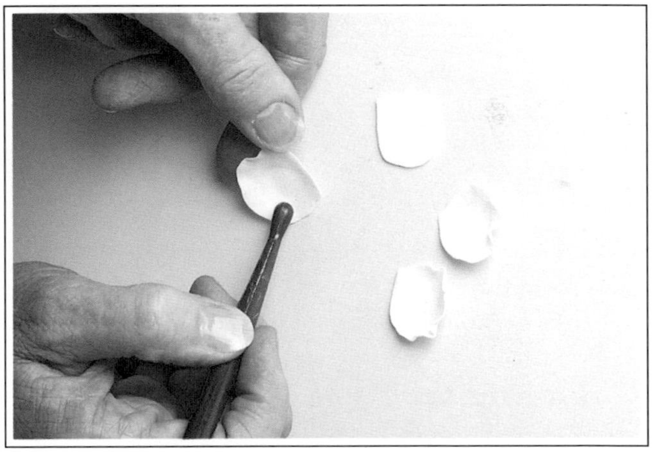

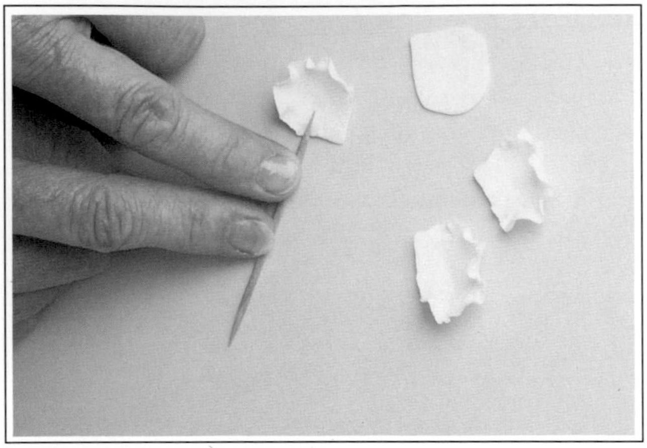

3 ❋ Flute the edge of the petal using a rounded toothpick (wooden pick), then cup the petal as in point 1.

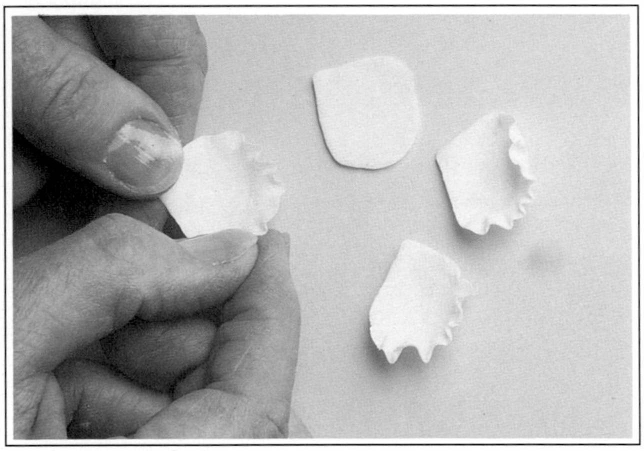

4 ❋ Flute the edges of the petal with your fingers, then form into a cup shape.
Leave completed petals to dry.

Colouring the Petal

You can make the petal in coloured paste or in white paste which you colour later. Use food colouring mixed with pure alcohol, vodka, gin or even cooking vodka. When colouring the centre of the flower, colour the bottom half of the petal from the pointed end upwards. Then without delay, using your thumb or finger, gently rub the colour in to avoid a watermark where the colour stops.

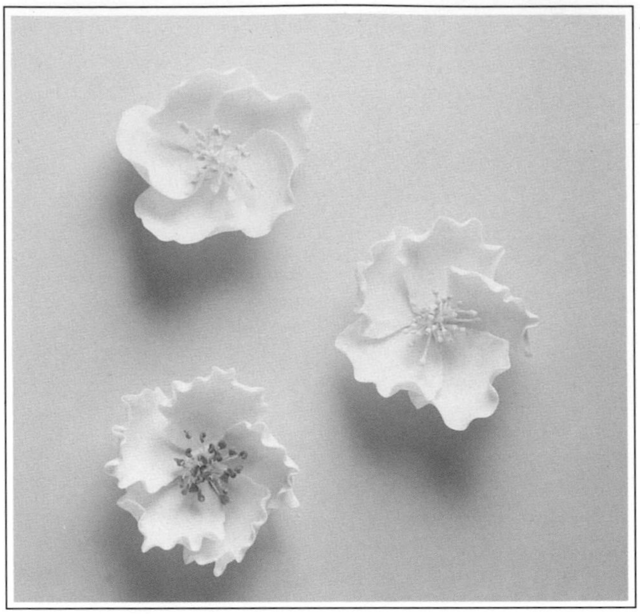

Assembling the Flower

Always work on waxed paper. This gives support and enables the flower to be peeled away easily when dry. Put a dab of royal icing in the middle of a 7 cm (2½ in) square of waxed paper. Place the point of the first petal in the royal icing, then add the remaining 4 petals, overlapping them slightly as you go.

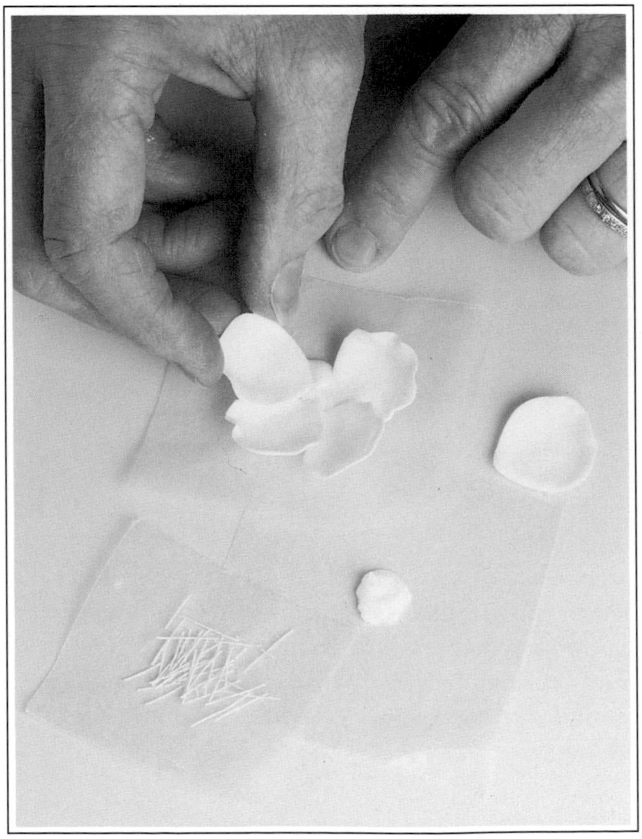

Tuck the last one under the edge of the first one. Remove any excess royal icing and fill this area with stamens, one at a time. Use a lot of stamens. A double Dainty Bess has a second roll of smaller petals inside the first row.

LILIES

The arum lily is white with a yellow tongue. The yellow lily is white with touches of green and a darker yellow tongue. The petals of the chestnut-brown lily are a pale plum colour inside and chestnut-brown outside. The tongue is pale yellow. You can use these lilies together in a spray or singly to expand a spray of other flowers.

PROBLEMS

1 ✽ If you have pressed the petal into a long, narrow shape rather than a square one, trim the bottom half into shape.

2 ✽ If the paste has become dry and cracked, you have been handling it for too long. Discard this piece and start again with fresh paste.

3 ✽ If the sides of the petal are folded, your left hand was not loose enough when cupping it.

4 ✽ If the cup shape looks stiff and unnatural, place the ball of your finger closer to the top edge of the petal and cup again.

5 ✽ Can you see royal icing around the inserted stamens? If so, you have not removed enough excess icing before inserting the stamens. When you look into the flower it should be neat and tidy.

ARUM LILY

Tongue

1 ✽ Make a tongue from yellow modelling paste.

2 ✽ Wire it and lightly cover the whole tongue with egg white.

3 ✽ Dip it into yellow, powdered, non-toxic chalk or petal dust and allow to dry.

Flower

1 ✲ Make a petal from a long bean of white modelling paste (about 2½ cm (1 in)) and shape to a point at both ends. Flatten.

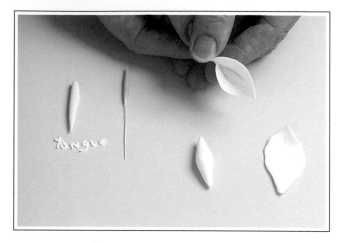

2 ✲ Wet the centre with a little water in a thin line from the middle of the petal to its base. Place the dry, wired tongue along the wet area, starting about a third of the way down the petal.

3 ✲ Wrap the bottom right side of the petal over the bottom half of the tongue and secure it in place with a touch of water.

4 ✲ Fold the left side over and neaten it down onto the wire.

5 ✲ Gently ease the top point of the petal back a little.

YELLOW LILY

Make in the same way as for the arum lily, but place the tongue lower down the petal and keep the fold lines to the centre when you wrap the petals over the tongue. Gently pinch the top of the petal and pull back to extend it. Tip the pinched point of the petal with green and apply a soft green water-wash to the back of the flower from the base to the tip.

CHESTNUT-BROWN LILY

Make the tongue longer and thinner than for the other 2 lilies. Fold the edges of the petals over the tongue, keeping the fold to the centre. Colour the outside of the flower with chestnut-brown non-

toxic chalk and the inside with light plum non-toxic chalk. Apply a wash of green up the back of the flower from the base to the tip. Look through your gardening books to find other colours that are easy to reproduce.

OPEN ROSE

This flower should not be confused with a double Dainty Bess. The open rose has 5 rows of petals. There are 3 small petals in the innermost row, 4 slightly larger ones in the next row, and so on. The number of petals increases by one for each row and they become slightly larger in size, until the outer row, which has large petals. The centre of the flower is filled with stamens.

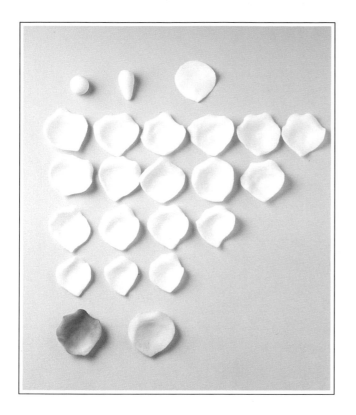

Method

Study the shape of a real rose petal. It is not deeply concave. Also note the way the petals fit together. You will need 25 petals for each rose, so estimate the amount of modelling paste you will require as accurately as you can. Model the 3 small petals first and put them to one side. Model the four larger petals for the next row and put them aside as a separate group. Do the same with the 5, 6 and 7 petals needed for the other rows. Leave them all to dry.

The method used to model the petals is the same for all sizes:

1 ✳ Take a bean of white modelling paste and flatten it between thumb and forefinger, keeping the shape reasonably square.

2 ✳ Place the paste petal over the pad of your thumb so that a 3 mm (⅛ in) overhang is left at the top.

3 ✳ Take the overhang gently between the thumb and forefinger of your other hand and turn it back, away from the thumb holding the petal. Do this in 2 or 3 different places. Do not pinch the paste. Make the curve smooth. Place the petal on the workbench (counter). It will have the shallow concave shape of a real rose petal.

Assembly

1 ✳ Press an 8 cm (3 in) square of waxed paper into one of the cups of a patty tin (pan).

2 ✳ Using a No 5 star tube, make a circle of royal icing, about 2½ cm (1 in) in size, in the centre.

3 ✳ Place the 7 outside petals in the royal icing, with the curved edge to the outside. Arrange so that they fit against each other and are standing up a little rather than lying flat.

4 ✳ Keeping the slightly upright angle, add the other petals one row at a time. Leave enough room in the centre for the stamens.

5 ✳ Use the thread of the stamen. Tip it with a darker colour. Work as quickly and efficiently as you can so that the royal icing does not dry before you have finished.

Colouring

I coloured the petals of the roses in the photographs (see above) before they were assembled. For the darker rose, the back and front of each petal was coloured using yellow non-toxic chalk, with pink non-toxic chalk darkening the outer edge, and yellow placed at the centre tip.

The lighter one was painted with food colouring mixed with pure alcohol. The petals are yellow, the tips shaded to pink.

ROSE MADE ON A PLASTIC MOULD

This method is ideal for beginners. Not only is it easy, but by using it, you really learn how a rose is constructed. You need a plastic sweetheart rose — most chain-stores have them. If you buy two, you can use one to make the moulds and keep the other as a guide.

Method

1 ✿ Pull the plastic rose apart and lay the petals on the workbench (counter), keeping the ones from each row together.
2 ✿ Inspect each petal and remove any protruding bits of plastic. Dust each one on both sides with cornflour (US cornstarch).
3 ✿ Pat out a ball of modelling paste as thin as possible. Take a small piece of paste and one plastic petal. Lightly press the paste onto the petal and cut away any excess around the edges. You may find that the edge of the petal will do the cutting for you.

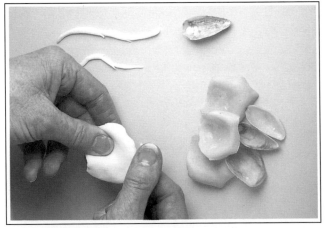

4 ✿ Lift the paste petal out of the plastic one. Re-dust the plastic petal with cornflour and replace the paste petal in it.
5 ✿ Continue in the same way for the remaining petals. Group each row of petals together on the workbench. Leave to dry. Always make 1 extra centre petal as 3 petals will not fold into a tight centre as well as 4.

Assembly

1 ✤ Place a dab of icing at the base of each of the 4 centre petals. Using the icing as 'cement', fit the 4 petals together and hold in place for about 5 seconds.

2 ✤ Turn the shape bottom-side up and fill the gaps with royal icing. This step is very important. The centre will be the basis for the remaining petals. Allow it to dry thoroughly before proceeding to the next row.

3 ✤ Keep an eye on your sample rose and notice how the petals fit next to each other. Add each row of petals using the same method.

4 ✤ Make sure the icing used for each row is thoroughly dry before you go on to the next row. It should be kept at the base of the petals and should not be seen when you look down into the rose.

5 ✤ When the rose is assembled, put it in the cup of a patty tin (pan) and leave to stand for 24 hours.

Colouring

A rose has a basic colour — white, pink, red — but the petals can be tinged with other colours or carry deeper tones of their own. You can colour the petals in different ways.

1 ✤ You can mould the petals in modelling paste that has been coloured pink, cream or red, then use chalks to make the lighter or darker markings.

2 ✤ You can use white modelling paste to make the petals, then colour them with chalk, liquid food colouring or petal dust. The paste petals must be left to dry for 24 hours before colouring of any sort is undertaken.

Note

When you can make this rose successfully, you can go on to making a standard rose. In the meantime you will find this one very attractive when arranged with a moulded bud, stalks and leaves.

PRIMULA

Primulas are small flowers, easy to make, and are used mainly as filler flowers. They come in mauve, purple, pink or white. They have a tiny speck of yellow in the centre.

Method

1 ✤ Shape a 6 mm (¼ in) bean-shaped piece of modelling paste into a cone.

2 ✤ Using a round toothpick (wooden pick), hollow out the cone.

3 ✤ Make 5 short cuts in the rim of the cone to form 5 petals of equal size.

4 ✤ With the open blade of your scissors, press a dent into the centre of the rim of each petal.

5 ✻ Round the top of the petals using thumb and forefinger. Flatten each one slightly. You now have 5 heart-shaped petals.

6 ✻ Wire the flower through the centre. Push the centre of the flower up a little and flatten back the petals to make a shallow cup. If you make the flower this way, you will not have to mitre the petals.

Colouring

1 ✻ Colour the centre of the flower yellow with food colouring straight from the bottle. Leave to dry thoroughly, otherwise it will 'bleed' into the colour of the petals.

2 ✻ Mix violet food colouring with pure alcohol and paint the back of each petal. The colour will seep through the paste and tint the upper side.

Assembly

The primula bud is small and bulbous. A grouping of 3 flowers and a bud make a nice spray.

VERBENA

The darker shades of the verbena make it a very useful filler flower for sprays of larger, darker flowers. All verbena flowers have a yellow-specked centre and a white eye, so always make them in white modelling paste.

Method

1 ✱ Take a small, bean-shaped piece of paste about 6 mm (¼ in) long. Mould it into a small cone.
2 ✱ Hollow out the centre with a round toothpick (wooden pick).
3 ✱ Make 5 short cuts of equal length in the rim of the cone to form 5 equal-sized petals.

4 ✱ Holding the flower, open the petals slightly and dent each one once with the blade of a pair of open scissors or a knife. Make sure the dent is in the centre of the petal.

5 ✱ Press the top corners of the petals gently with your fingers, then flatten each petal. You will now have a flower with 5 heart-shaped petals.

6 ⁑ Using a very small ball tool, make the centre of the flower quite deep.

7 ⁑ Wire using a very small hook at the head of the wire, and allow to dry.

Colouring

1 ⁑ Use food colouring either mixed with water or pure alcohol.

2 ⁑ Paint the back of the petals with a lighter shade of the main colour. Allow to dry.

3 ⁑ Paint in the yellow centre of the flower. Allow to dry.

4 ⁑ Paint the front of the petal with the main colour. Leave a white eye around the hollowed centre and work from the centre to the edge of each petal.

Assembly

You are unlikely to need just 1 verbena. Make a number of them, paint in different colours and group into a spray.

BALLERINA ROSE

This climbing rose from the musk family flowers in huge clusters and is very easy to model. The delicate colouring makes it ideal for cake decoration. Always make it in white modelling paste and colour the back of the petals with food colouring mixed with pure alcohol. The colour will seep through the paste and give the flower its typical soft pink glow.

5 ✸ Take a small square of waxed paper. Mark one point Bb on point B to form a pleat. Hold the pleat in place with a dab of royal icing at this point.
6 ✸ Arrange the 5 petals in the royal icing, each one overlapping the next at the centre.

7 ✸ Fill the centre with yellow stamen threads tipped with brown. Use just enough royal icing to keep them firm, but no more.

Method

1 ✸ Make a 1 cm (½ in) bean-shaped piece of paste and flatten it slightly.
2 ✸ Indent the rounded edge in the centre to make a heart-shaped petal.
3 ✸ Flatten the petal again.
4 ✸ Make 4 more petals in exactly the same way. Curve the heart-shaped top slightly. Leave the petals to dry.

Colouring

1 ✸ Mix pink food colouring with pure alcohol.
2 ✸ Paint the back of each petal with a fine brush. Keep the colour strongest at the top of the petal.
3 ✸ Leave to dry.

Flower Making — Intermediate Level

HYACINTH

Although it is the most commonly used filler flower, the hyacinth is not easy to make. The method I describe below eliminates some of the mitring and shaping usually considered necessary. The flower has 6 petals and comes in several colours, including blue, one of the very few flowers in that shade to be used in cake decorating. You can make it in white paste then colour it with food colouring mixed with pure alcohol or make it in coloured paste.

ABOVE: *Crab apple*

Method

1 ❋ Hollow out a small bean of white paste with a round toothpick (wooden pick) to make a small cone.

2 ❋ Using scissors, cut from the rim of the cone to within a third of the base.

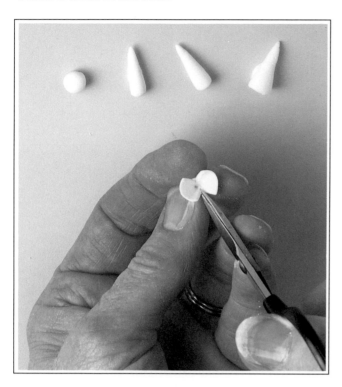

3 ❋ Make a second cut opposite the first one.

4 ❋ The cone now has 2 halves. Make 3 deep cuts in each half so that you have 6 petals.

5 ❋ Snip off the top corners of each petal.

6 ❋ Mark the centre of each petal lengthwise with the back of a knife or scissors.

7 ❋ Squeeze the point of each petal, flatten, then gently squeeze again. Bend each petal outwards very slightly. Do not pinch the whole petal or the flower will end up looking like a spider.

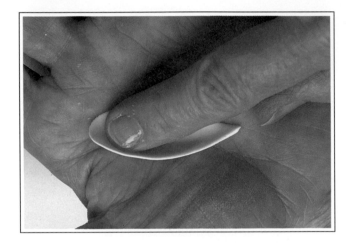

8 ✳ Wire the flower and gently deepen the centre.

Colouring

1 ✳ Mix blue colour with pure alcohol and paint the back of the flowers only.

2 ✳ The colour seeps through and gives the flower a delicate look.

FRANGIPANI

Some people seem to have trouble with the petal shape of this lovely flower, but you will find the following method very easy. Make the flower in white paste and colour it once it is dry.

Method

1 ✳ Take a bean of paste about 2½ cm (1 in) long. Shape it so that it tapers to a point at the bottom and is nicely rounded at the top.

2 ✳ Flatten into shape.

3 ✳ There are 2 possible methods for carrying out the next step:

(a) Shape the petal. Place it in your left hand, just below the pad of the thumb. Run your finger down the length of the petal, exerting gentle pressure — just enough to make the edge of the top side bend slightly inwards.

(b) Place the petal along the inside of your fore-

finger. Now place your thumb along the petal, leaving a small margin of paste protruding above your thumb. Roll that small margin towards the thumb. You will now have a turned edge across the top and down the left-hand side of the petal.

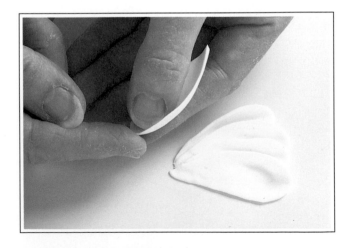

4 ✳ Make another 4 petals in exactly the same way.

5 ✳ Wet each petal on the right-hand side (the one that is not curled) to about a quarter of the way up the petal.

6 ✳ Keeping the top of the petals level, lay the second petal on the first, the third on the second, the fourth on the third and the fifth on the fourth, overlapping them as in the photograph opposite.

7 ✳ Pick up the joined petals. Wet the right-hand side of the fifth petal to about a quarter of the way up. Wrap it around the back of the first petal to overlap by about one-third.

8 ✳ Roll the bottom of the flower, where the thinnest part of the petals join, between thumb and forefinger, squeezing gently to make sure they hold together. This should make a slight spiral at the centre of the flower.

9 ✳ Hold the flower upright and coax the petals out to resemble the frangipani's shape.

10 ✳ To support the flower while it dries, insert into a hollow, plastic bottle-stopper. If you cut the stoppers at different heights, the shape of the flowers can be varied. A lower support will result in a more open flower.

Colouring

When completely dry, colour the centre with an old brush dipped in yellow chalk. It is safer to use dry colour because liquid colour may seep up the petal and leave a watermark.

SWEET PEA

The sweet pea is simple to make, and since it comes in both dark and delicately pale colours, it is very useful for a spray. Use white modelling paste rolled as thinly as possible to keep the ethereal look of the flower. I use British paper-covered wire when making this flower to give the head extra support.

Method

1 ✳ Take a pea-sized piece of modelling paste and shape it into a crescent.

2 ✳ Insert a tightly hooked piece of wire into one of the pointed ends of the crescent and leave to dry.

3 ✳ Make a Dainty Bess-shaped petal (see p 35). Widen it slightly with a small rolling pin. Flute the edges using your fingers.

4 ✳ Wet the back of the wired crescent and wrap the petal round it. Neaten the join at the base and curve the petal so that it stands up and out a little.

5 ✳ Make a second Dainty Bess petal, larger and wider than the first one. Flute the edges with your fingers.

6 ✳ Wet the bottom half of the larger petal in the centre. Wrap it around the smaller petal and ease it back away from that petal, which encircles the crescent.

Colouring

Using an atomiser that gives a fine spray, spray the whole flower with food colouring mixed with pure alcohol.

CARNATION

The carnation is a bulky flower, so the modelling paste must be as thin as possible. To shape the flower, I use a spiked flower holder with a 5 x 5 cm (2 x 2 in) square block of Plasticine pressed down onto the spikes. I insert an old piping tube into this, then press a square of aluminium foil into the tube with my little finger. I shape the aluminium foil protruding from the top of the tube so that it will support the petals of the flower I am about to make.

Flower

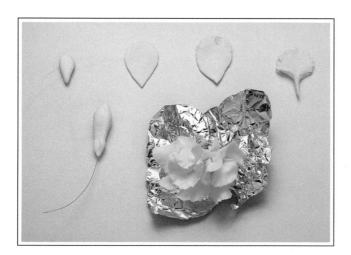

1 ✢ Take a 1 cm (½ in) bean of modelling paste and flatten it into a teardrop shape. Flute the top edge with your fingers. Don't worry if you tear it — this makes the petal look more natural. Make approximately 12 petals.

2 ✢ Wet the aluminium foil at the base of the tube. Insert the pointed end of the petal and ease the top back over the foil.

3 ✢ Insert the next petal so that it slightly overlaps the first. Continue inserting petals around the tube until a slightly oval shape is formed.
4 ✢ Make a second row of petals in between the ones in the row before and keep them slightly upright.

51

5 ✽ Continue inserting petals, working towards the centre, until the centre is full of petals which create a slightly domed effect. It should not be flat.

6 ✽ The flowers can be coloured red, pink, magenta, yellow or similar shades, but not blue. Use food colouring straight from the bottle or mixed with pure alcohol.

Calyx

1 ✽ Hollow a 2½ cm (1 in) cone of white modelling paste and made 5 short cuts in the rim.

2 ✽ Mitre each sepal and flatten slightly.

3 ✽ If you wish to wire the flower, insert the wire now and attach the calyx to the back of the flower by slightly dampening the inside of the cone. Alternatively, make the calyx and, while still damp, attach it to the dried flower.

Leaves

The colour of the calyx and the leaves is a green I have always found difficult to mix. Try a leaf-green shade mixed with blue, and add a speck of black. The easiest way to make a leaf is to roll out the modelling paste and press a real leaf into it. Use it as a guide, trimming and shaping around it. Never leave a leaf flat.

VIOLET

The easiest way to make a violet is in one piece from a cone of paste. They have a little white face in the centre, so use white modelling paste and then colour afterwards. Violets are not always deep purple; they can be a much paler, softer shade, so vary the colouring when you make a spray of violets.

Flower

1 ✽ Hollow out a ½ cm (¼ in) cone of white paste using a hair-roller pin.

2 ✽ Make a long cut into the rim. Make a slightly shorter cut on either side, close enough to form 2 'ears'. Gently turn back the ears.

3 ✽ Make a cut on either side of the ears to form a wider petal. This should take you slightly more than halfway down the circle.

4 ✽ Curve the bottom of the circle of paste outwards to form the bottom petal of the violet.

5 ✽ Mitre the ears and flatten slightly.

5 ✣ When it is dry, paint it yellow-orange.

6 ✣ Paint a tiny leaf-green calyx on the outside of the flower.

TUBEROSE

6 ✣ Mitre the side petals, maintaining their width. Flatten and twist gently sideways — not a lot, just enough to take the flatness out of the flower.

7 ✣ Using the round end of the hair-roller pin, curve the bottom petal slightly upwards.

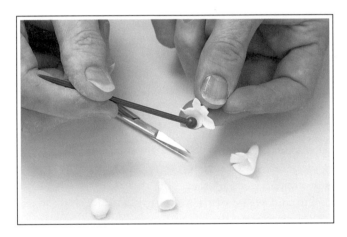

Most brides like to have a tuberose in their bouquet, so why not on the cake? This is not a filler flower. It is large enough for 1 flower and 1 bud to make a spray. It can be made in white modelling paste and coloured later, or in cream-coloured paste.

Bud

1 ✣ Shape a long thin bud onto the end of a wire and flatten slightly. Allow to firm in place.

2 ✣ Curve the wire so that the bud faces downwards.

Colouring

1 ✣ Use food colouring straight from the bottle to paint the back of the flowers.

2 ✣ Leave a white area at the base of each petal to form the central eye of the violet. Paint the front of the petal from the eye outwards, making certain the edges of the petal are coloured. Leave to dry.

3 ✣ Using a non-toxic cake decorating pen, draw tiny black stripes in the white area of the bottom petal.

4 ✣ Pipe a dot of royal icing in the centre of the flower and 'pull' it to make a longish stamen.

Flower

1 ✽ Shape a long bud of modelling paste on the end of a knotted or hooked piece of wire and make firm.

2 ✽ Hollow out a 1 cm (½ in) long cone with a hair-roller pin. Make the cavity wide enough to be able to fit another row of petals and the bud.

3 ✽ Make 5 long cuts around the rim to make 5 petals. Mitre each one, flatten, and gently curve outwards.

4 ✽ Make a second but slightly smaller cone (½ cm (¼ in) long) and make another 5 petals in the same way. Cut off the base of this cone and fit it into the first cone. Wet the back of the petals and arrange them so that they alternate with those of the first cone.

5 ✽ Insert the wired bud in the centre of the 2 cones and gently mould the whole flower into shape. Cut off any excess paste at the base of the first cone and smooth onto the wire. Leave to dry.

Bud

Mould a long (1½ cm (⅜ in)), bulbous, heavy bud of paste onto the end of a hooked piece of wire.

Colouring

1 ✽ Colour the flower dark cream with liquid food colouring or non-toxic chalk. Start at the centre, and shade to light cream at the edges of the petals.

2 ✽ Colour the buds cream with brownish-pink tips.

LITTLE MINT LADIES

These small flowers are like an open bell; they have wide petals and a striated or spotted throat. The red, purple, lilac, mauve, pink, greenish-yellow, cream and white of their colouring make them very useful as a spray flower or for use with orchids.

Basic Bell

1 ✽ Hollow out a 2 cm (¾ in) cone of paste with a No 2 former tool and ease out the bottom half of the cone so that a bell shape is formed.

2 ✽ Make 3 long cuts in the lower half of the rim to make 3 petals.

3 ✽ Make 2 long cuts in the upper rim to make 2 petals.

4 ✽ Round the top of the lower petals. Gently elongate and flatten the whole of these petals.

5 ✽ Mitre the top petals. Flatten the whole of each petal and gently roll the top outwards.

6 ✽ Reshape the bell with a No 4 former tool.

7 ✽ Flute the bottom petals outwards, using a round toothpick (wooden pick).

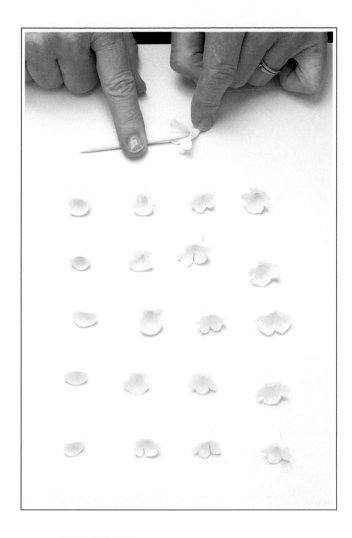

Blue Mist Lady

1 ✳ Make as for the basic bell but with 3 cuts in the lower rim of the cone.

2 ✳ Round and flatten the petals so that they almost meet.

3 ✳ Mix some violet food colouring and a touch of blue food colouring with pure alcohol. Paint first the back of the flower, then the front.

4 ✳ Use deep purple chalk to colour the centre.

Mountain Mist Lady

1 ✳ Make the basic bell, but roll the top petals inwards so that they face each other.

2 ✳ Cut the lower rim of the cone so that it has a narrow petal on either side of the wider one.

3 ✳ Indent the bottom centre of the wide petal and, using a round toothpick (wooden pick), roll it backwards.

4 ✳ Cut the 2 narrow petals to about half their length. Flatten gently and ease out sideways.

5 ✳ Colour the centre of the flower with mauve chalk.

6 ✳ Dot the bottom petals with a tangerine non-toxic colouring pen. The dots should go down into the bell.

7 ✳ Put 2 small tangerine strips on the side petals.

Silver Mint Lady

1 ✳ Make the bell with all the petals facing inwards.

2 ✳ Roll the 3 bottom petals upwards, using a round toothpick (wooden pick).

3 ✳ Paint the centre of the flower with yellow chalk, taking the colour down onto the centre bottom petal.

4 ✳ Mix some pink-mauve food colouring with pure alcohol and paint first the back of the flower, then the front. Go over the lower edges of the petals a second time with this colour.

Chinese Mint Lady

1 ✳ Make the basic bell, but with the petals all the same size.

2 ✳ Round the tops and ball each petal (see p 5) from the back.

3 ✳ Re-form the centre of the flower with a ball tool.

4 ✳ Paint the petals with pink food colouring mixed with pure alcohol.

Peppermint Lady

1 ✳ Make as for the basic bell and allow to dry.

2 ✳ Colour the centre with yellow chalk.

3 ✳ Using a non-toxic colouring pen, cover the top petals with tiny rows of grape-violet dots, working from the centre out.

Assembly

Each flower should be wired. For a spray, you will need 3–6 flowers.

DAFFODIL

These flowers must be made from paste rolled as thinly as possible, otherwise they will look ugly and bulky. They can be made with white paste and coloured when dry, or with paste to which lemon and a little orange food colouring has been added.

Back Petals

1 ✤ Using a daffodil cutter, cut 3 petals and finger the edges.
2 ✤ Roll each petal out, lengthways first, then crossways.
3 ✤ Press crepe paper onto the petals so that the paper's indentations give the paste a natural look.
4 ✤ Use a Plasticine block with an aluminium foil insert (see p 51). Arrange the 3 petals in the foil and ease the centre down with a No 2 former tool.

5 ✤ Cut a second set of 3 petals and repeat steps 2 and 3.
6 ✤ Place the second row of petals inside the first row of petals, alternating the petals in each row. Leave to dry in the holder.

Trumpet

1 ❋ Make a cone of paste approximately two-thirds the size of the finished flower — you know what a daffodil looks like.

2 ❋ Pinch out the top edge of the cone and flute, using either your fingers or a round toothpick (wooden pick).

3 ❋ Insert the bottom of a No 3 former tool into the cone and open it up into a bell-shaped trumpet.

4 ❋ Wet the bottom of the trumpet with water and place it in the centre of the petals in the holder.

5 ❋ Fix 3–4 yellow stamens into place using a dab of royal icing.

Calyx

1 ❋ Make a calyx of 5 sepals from paste that is coloured pale green.

2 ❋ Wire the calyx.

3 ❋ Wet the cup of the calyx and insert the dried flower.

SWEETHEART ROSE

The subtle colouring of this rose's petals makes it particularly interesting. You will need white, pink and yellow paste. The petals in the outer row are white, those in the second row are yellow and white, those in the third are pink and white, and the centre ones are pink and yellow.

To achieve the delicate colour combination, take a small ball of white paste and an equal-sized ball of yellow paste and wedge them together. Rub gently to combine the colours until the white is at the top of the petal and the yellow at the bottom, with no defined point where the colours change. Repeat this process with white and pink paste and pink and yellow paste. You will need approximately 7–8 petals to form the outer row of the flower. Use as many other petals as necessary to fill in the middle.

I make this flower on a ring of paste so that the outer petals are supported. Otherwise, it can look flat and uninteresting.

Method

1 ✣ Roll a piece of paste about 8 cm (3 in) long and 3 mm (⅛ in) thick. Shape it into a ring. Allow to dry thoroughly.

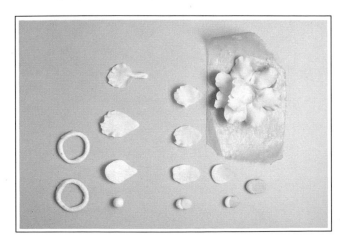

2 ✣ The petals are teardrop in shape, about 2½ cm (1 in) long and 1 cm (½ in) wide. Flute the top edges with your fingers and pleat the bottom.

3 ✣ Place the ring on a square of waxed paper and arrange the outer row of white petals. Attach the petals individually to the paper with a small drop of water. Fold each petal over the ring so that it overlaps the previous one. Flatten the base of the petals. The central area should be as open as possible, with enough space for the inner rows of petals. You can support the white petals with little pads of waxed paper to help keep their shape.

4 ✣ Insert the white and yellow petals, keeping the yellow at the base. Cup them so that they stand up, then ease the upper half of the petals back over the first row.

5 ✣ Insert the white and pink petals inside the second row, with the pink portion at the base. Keep them standing up.

6 ✣ Fill the centre of the flower with the pink and yellow petals — either colour can be at the top.

ABELIA

This small flower can be used on its own or in a cluster. The pale mauve bell has a tiny, pale cinnamon calyx; the leaves are multicoloured.

Flower

1 ✻ Make a cone about 1 cm (½ in) long from a piece of white paste.
2 ✻ Hollow out with a hair-roller pin and make 5 short cuts around the rim to make 5 petals.
3 ✻ Trim around the top of the petals. Flatten them gently.
4 ✻ Using a ball tool, enlarge the hollowed base of the cone to make it bell-shaped.
5 ✻ Run the ball tool up the back of each petal and curve the edges outwards.
6 ✻ Insert wire in the flower.
7 ✻ Mix the palest mauve food colouring (it must not be violet) with pure alcohol. Paint the back of the flower, deepening the tone slightly down one side towards the bottom. Leave to dry.
8 ✻ Using a tiny blossom cutter, cut a calyx from cinnamon-coloured paste. Attach to the flower with a touch of water.
9 ✻ Put a small spot of royal icing into the throat of the bell and insert 4 stamens. Allow them to protrude slightly from the bell.

Buds

1 ✻ Mould a small piece of paste onto the end of a piece of wire to make a small, bulbous bud.
2 ✻ Paint a darker shade of mauve than the flower.

Leaves

1 ✻ Make a small, oval, pointed leaf in green paste.
2 ✻ Splash with a russet-brown food colouring mixed with water.
3 ✻ Insert wire.

Assembly

When assembling a spray, make sure that the darker coloured buds complement the flower, but do not dominate the spray.

TIGER LILY

1 ✥ Using beans of modelling paste, shape 6 petals approximately 5 cm (2 in) long, with a softly pointed tip and a long, tapering 'tail'.

2 ✥ Flatten each petal.

3 ✥ Pull out, curve and twist the tail just a little.

4 ✥ Widen each petal from the base to halfway up the petal.

5 ✥ Flute each side of the upper part of the petals.

6 ✥ Using a knife, make a gentle depression in the centre of each petal from the base to three-quarters of the way up the petal.

7 ✥ Cut a circle of aluminium foil. Insert the foil into a tube in a Plasticine block. Press it down into the base and out against the sides, and smooth the surplus at the rim out into a circle.

If you follow the instructions you can make any species of *Lilium*, just vary the colouring as needed. Work in white paste and colour the parts when dry. Make 1 petal at a time and dry each one separately. Tiger lilies have 6 hammerhead stamens and 1 anther with a knob end.

Flower

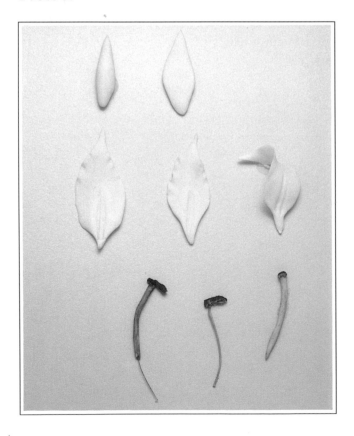

8 ✥ Place each petal in the aluminium foil tube in the following order and position:
    petal 1 at 12 o'clock
    petal 2 at 7 o'clock
    petal 3 at 5 o'clock
    petal 4 at 2 o'clock

petal 5 at 6 o'clock
petal 6 at 10 o'clock.

When placing the petals in position, shape and twist them back a little. Make sure you leave the centre open, and that it is deep enough to take 6 stamens and 1 anther. Do not allow the petals to touch one another. Leave to dry with the foil providing a support.

Colouring

1 ✤ Colour each petal separately.
2 ✤ For an orange tiger lily, mix orange food colouring with pure alcohol. Wash all over the back and front of the petal and allow to dry thoroughly.
3 ✤ Using a darker shade of orange make a wash down the centre of each petal. Allow to dry.
4 ✤ The markings on the throat of the petals can be made in 2 different ways:

Use a fine paintbrush to make tiny dots in a darker shade of orange. Then smudge them into the colour of the petal with a half-dry brush.

Pipe many tiny dots of royal icing onto the petal and paint them a dark orange when the icing is dry.

The lily in the photographs was coloured with a wash of orange food colouring and a touch of peach, mixed with pure alcohol.

Stamens and Anther

These must be carefully made. You can use wire with a small head of paste or make them completely from paste.
1 ✤ Roll the paste out as thin as a round toothpick (wooden pick).
2 ✤ Form the hammerhead stamens by folding back half the paste at the top, flattening it, then shaping it into a curve. Dry this flat.

3 ✤ Shape the anther so that it is straighter and longer, with a flat, knobbed top.
4 ✤ Paint and dry the stamens and anther.
5 ✤ Insert them in the flower carefully, using a little royal icing to hold them in place.

CRAB APPLE

The unusual burgundy colouring of this flower ranges from dark burgundy for the buds and small flowers to a very pale burgundy for the larger flowers. It is important to note that the flowers are white inside and are only coloured on the underside.

Flower

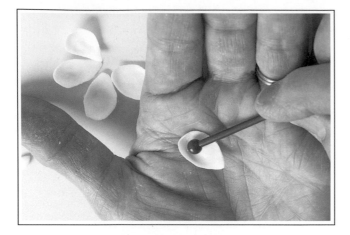

1 ✠ Make a bean of white paste 6 mm (¼ in) long. Flatten it, keeping the point to the bottom.
2 ✠ Cup the edges gently and leave the petal to dry.
3 ✠ Make 5 of these petals for each flower.
4 ✠ Place a small dot of royal icing onto a small square of waxed paper.
5 ✠ Place the 5 petals in the royal icing so that each one overlaps at the point. Make some flowers with the petals half-closed and others that are fully opened. Allow to dry.
6 ✠ Fill the centres with half-headed cream stamens.

Buds

1 ✠ Make a number of bulbous buds in graduating sizes and at different stages of opening.
2 ✠ Insert in separately made calyxes and hold in place with royal icing.
3 ✠ Wire and allow to dry.

Colouring

Paint the buds and flowers with non-toxic chalk or petal dust. Match the right colour using the real flower as a guide.

Leaves

1 ✠ Make an oval leaf approximately 1¼ cm (½ in) long in the same shape as the sweet apple leaf.
2 ✠ Finely serrate the edges and dry fairly flat.
3 ✠ Colour a pale apple-green.
Use plenty of buds when making the spray.

OPPOSITE: *Daphne*

Flower Making —
Advanced Level

FUCHSIA

Fuchsias are not the easiest flowers to make. Because they can be bulky, it's important to keep your paste as finely moulded as possible. Their strong natural colours can be a bit heavy, so create a paler colour theme of your own. Make them in white paste and colour later.

Method — Large Single Fuchsia

1 ✠ Wire 6 stamens together and cover the wire twist with a tiny strip of Stemtex.

2 ✠ Make a small petal in a Dainty Bess shape (see p 35). Cup it quite deeply.

3 ✠ Make 3 more petals.

4 ❋ Moisten each one from the pointed end to about halfway up the petal. Join the petals together so that they overlap slightly.

5 ❋ Wet the back of the first petal and bring the fourth petal around to form a bell. Press together.
6 ❋ Pull the wired stamens through and neaten the bottom of the bell onto the wire. Leave to dry.
7 ❋ To make the calyx, hollow out a 2 cm (¾ in) cone of paste and make 4 long cuts into the rim for 4 sepals.

8 ❋ Mitre each sepal into a neat leaf shape.
9 ❋ Slip the calyx up the wire and attach it to the back of the bell with a dab of water. Neaten it onto the wire.
10 ❋ Make sure the calyx fits neatly over and down onto the bell shape.
11 ❋ Paint the flower using one colour for the bell and a deeper or paler shade for the calyx. The small bud ending of the calyx, which fits into the wire, should be pale green.

Method — Double Fuchsia

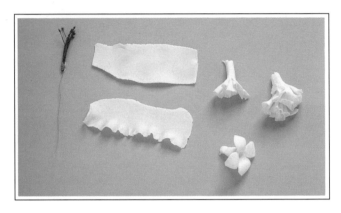

1 ❋ Wire 6 stamens together and cover the wire with a tiny strip of Stemtex.
2 ❋ Roll out a piece of white modelling paste as thinly as possible to approximately 2½ x 5 cm (1 x 2 in).
3 ❋ Flute 1 long edge. Now concertina the piece, using a little water to hold the folds in place.

4 ❋ Using a second piece of paste, make an identical piece.

5 ✠ Use water to join the 2 pieces together down the long edge. Shape into a bell.

6 ✠ Insert the wired stamen in the bell. Neaten the back and leave the flower to dry.

7 ✠ Hollow out a 2½ cm (1 in) cone of paste. Make 4 long cuts in the rim to form 4 petals.

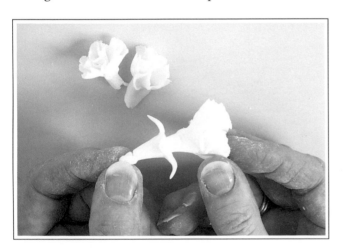

8 ✠ Mitre the corners of each petal and broaden the centre by flattening and turning back the edges.

9 ✠ Insert the piece of wire holding the bell into this flower shape. Pull the shape up the wire and neaten onto the back of the bell.

10 ✠ Squeeze the junction very gently and mark with a knife to make a small, bulbous ending to the flower.

11 ✠ Mix pale mauve or pink food colouring with pure alcohol. Paint the flower. Make the outer rim of the petals a darker shade of the same colour and the small, bulbous ending a pale green. You can also paint the wire green or brown.

Method — Tiny Single Fuchsia

1 ✠ Wire 4 stamens together and cover the wire twist with a small strip of Stemtex.

2 ✠ Hollow out a cone of white modelling paste 1 cm (½ in) long with a toothpick (wooden pick).

3 ✠ Make 4 long cuts into the rim to form 4 petals.

4 ✠ Round and slightly flatten each petal.

5 ✠ Use a No 2 ball tool to bell out each petal by rolling lengthways and sideways.

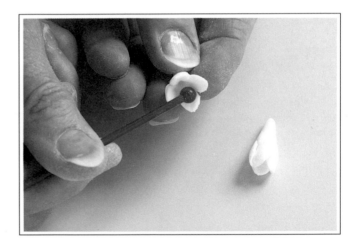

6 ✠ Make a bell from the 4 petals by overlapping each one.

7 ✠ Pull the stamens onto the wire through the bell.

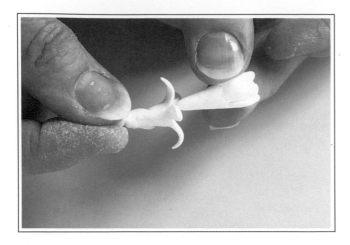

8 ✱ Cut a 4-petal calyx as for the other 2 fuchsias, but make the petals longer and thinner. Insert the wire and draw the calyx up to the small bell. Pinch gently to make a bulbous ending.

9 ✱ Colour, using a lighter shade for petals and a darker shade for the calyx.

DAPHNE

This lovely, old-fashioned flower reminds me of my grandmother, so I feel it is just right for a cake for an elderly woman. I pulled the real flower to pieces many times before I found the right way of making it. The flowers in each head open at different times, so you can make your own decision about the numbers of buds, half-opened flowers and fully opened flowers to use in each head. I use a pale burgundy-pink paste and make about 20 buds, ranging from the very tiny to the half-open, 2 half-opened flowers, and 4–5 fully opened flowers.

Flowers

1 ✱ Hollow out a ½ cm (¼ in) cone of paste, keeping the tail of the cone long.

2 ✱ Make 2 long cuts in the rim to form 2 petals facing each other. Call these petals 1 and 2.

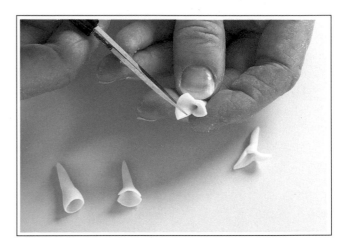

3 ✱ Cut 2 leaf-shaped petals with pointed tips. Call these petals 3 and 4. Attach each one with water between petals 1 and 2, at the side of the flower. Use a round toothpick (wooden pick) to gently roll them backwards, leaving petals 1 and 2 upright.

4 ✱ Insert a yellow-headed stamen in the centre of the flower. Hold in position with a tiny dot of royal icing.

5 ✱ Mix burgundy-pink with a touch of mauve food colouring in a little water. Lightly edge petals 1 and 2 with a very small amount of colour. Paint petals 3 and 4 all over the back and tail.

Buds

1 ✾ Make a long bean of paste with a thicker head. You will need many buds, so vary the size of the heads but always keep a long tail.

2 ✾ To make half a bud, flag out the top and wrap it around the bud.

3 ✾ Paint the bud burgundy, leaving a tiny amount of paste showing at the tip to represent the unopened flower.

Calyx

1 ✾ Hollow out a cone of green paste 2½ cm (1 in) long and widen the rim until it is about 2 cm (¾ in) in diameter.

2 ✾ Make short cuts around the rim and mitre the sepals.

3 ✾ While the paste is still wet, half-fill the calyx with royal icing. Fill with the buds, the half-opened buds and, lastly, the flowers. Tighten the calyx at the back but leave enough calyx to hold the head together. Leave to dry.

Leaves

Make the leaves in leaf-green paste and paint in the same colour when dry. If you cannot use the real leaf to imprint and shape the paste, cut a leaf shape that is pointed at both ends and wide at the centre, then mark in the veins.

Assembly

A spray of 3 heads with accompanying leaves is sufficient for a large cake.

GARDENIA

This beautiful white flower is not easy to make, and the paste must be as fine as possible. When the real flower opens, the outer 2 rows of petals flatten and curve downwards and the other petals open at different stages. When you are shaping the flower, bear this in mind.

Flower

1 ✾ Make a ring of white paste about 8 cm (3 in) long and 3 mm (⅛ in) thick. Dampen one end and attach to the other. Leave to dry thoroughly on a square of waxed paper.

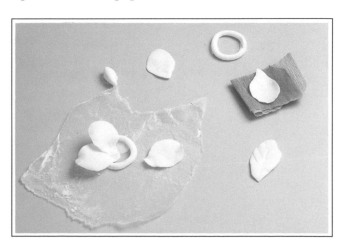

Leaves

1 ✳ If possible, use a real leaf to cut out the oval shape.
2 ✳ Cut the shape and finger gently.
3 ✳ Mark the centre vein with the back of a knife.
4 ✳ Put in the side markings with tweezers.
5 ✳ Mix leaf-green and yellow food colouring and add a touch of brown. Paint the leaves once they are dry.
6 ✳ When completely dry, rub the leaves with a speck of petroleum jelly (which is quite safe) to give them a dull shine.

Buds

These are very special and the shape must be copied from real buds. However, they are worth the effort as they make a spray look complete.

1 ✳ Make a 2½ cm (1 in) long bean of paste with a point at both ends.
2 ✳ Place tiny rolled pieces of paste at the base of the cone so that they stand out to form a calyx.
3 ✳ Paint the calyx and bud the same green as the leaves.

2 ✳ Make a petal in a Dainty Bess shape (see p 35). Ease the sides out slightly and bring the top up into a gently peak. Press onto a pad of crepe paper to give the petal texture. Make approximately 8 petals.
3 ✳ Dampen the waxed paper in the centre of the ring of paste. With a ball tool, arrange the petals around it, tail downwards and overlapping slightly. Do this until you have formed the outer ring of the flower. Do not allow the petals to lie flat. Ease into shape and support with waxed paper.
4 ✳ Make a second inner row of petals. If they need support, use waxed paper again.
5 ✳ Continue making rows of petals, allowing them to stand up more towards the centre of the flower.
6 ✳ Leave the centre open enough to place 3 small, yellow, V-shaped pieces inside.

STEPHANOTIS

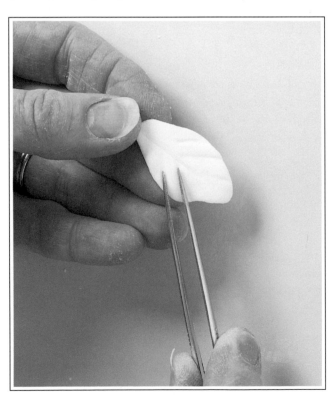

The his lovely flower makes an excellent decoration for a wedding cake.

Flower

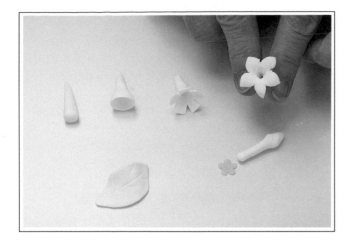

1 ✷ Hollow out a 2 cm (¾ in) long cone of white modelling paste.

2 ✷ Make 5 short cuts around the rim to create 5 equal-sized petals.

3 ✷ Round the edges of the petals.

4 ✷ Insert a ball tool right down into the bottom of the cone and gently shape the paste. Remove the tool and roll the central part of the cone between your fingers. The result should be petals at the top of the cone, a narrow section in the middle, and a bulb shape at the bottom.

5 ✷ Turn the flower over gently and ball (see p 5) the back of each petal. Turn right-side again and gently twist one or two of the petals.

6 ✷ Use a knotted wire to wire each flower.

7 ✷ Dust the back of the flower with yellow chalk to give a soft creamy look.

Buds

1 ✷ Make the bud with the same narrow middle section as the flower.

2 ✷ Mix cream food colouring and a touch of orange food colouring with pure alcohol. Paint from the top down, getting lighter towards the base.

Calyx

1 ✷ Cut a very tiny calyx with the smallest forget-me-not cutter.

2 ✷ Slip it up the wire and attach to the back of the flower with water.

Leaves

1 ✷ Cut the leaves from dark green paste.

2 ✷ Round them at the top and vein deeply.

3 ✷ Paint over with dark green food colouring mixed with pure alcohol.

Assembly

As a filler, 3 flowers and 3 buds will be enough. If used as a spray on its own, make any number of both.

BLACK-EYED SUSAN

The bright colour of this flower and the unusual shape of the bud make this a very effective cake decoration.

Flower

1 ✷ Make a cone of modelling paste 2½ cm (1 in) long with a diameter of 1¼ cm (½ in) at the rim end.

2 ✳ Using a No 3 former tool, hollow out the cone until the diameter of the opened rim is about 2½ cm (1 in).

3 ✳ Make 5 short cuts around the rim to create 5 petals.

4 ✳ Round the corners and then flatten each petal.

5 ✳ Immediately press petals into a pad of crepe paper to give a natural texture.

6 ✳ Join the tips of the thumb and forefinger of one hand together to make a circle. Drop the cone into it, pointed side down, with the petals lying out flat from the centre of the circle.

7 ✳ With your other hand, gently press and extend the bottom part of the cone to form a long tail. At the same time, gently squeeze the circle of your thumb and forefinger so that the centre of the flower narrows to a 5 mm (¼ in) diameter throat.

8 ✳ Insert a No 1 former tool into the centre of the flower and gently hollow it out.

Colouring

1 ✳ Mix orange food colouring and a touch of apricot or peach food colouring with pure alcohol.

2 ✳ Paint the front and back of the petals.

3 ✳ Paint the tail of the flower with mauve food colouring mixed with pure alcohol.

4 ✳ When the flower is completely dry, paint the centre of the flower — the 'black eye' — with violet food colouring straight from the bottle. It is essential that this colour should not run. The 'eye' should be in sharp contrast to the colour of the petals.

Buds

1 ✳ Make a cone of green paste and flatten the rim end into a square.

2 ✳ Invert it so that it stands on the square base.

3 ✳ Using a sharp knife, make a cut from the pointed end running two-thirds of the way down the cone.

4 ✳ Open the cut slightly and insert a hair-roller pin to keep it open.

5 ✳ Using tweezers, pinch a vertical ridge on either side of the cut.

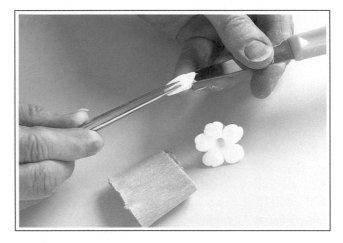

6 ✳ Replace the hair-roller pin with a knife. Keep the cut open while you work on the flat areas supported by the knife.

7 ✳ Make a vertical ridge with the tweezers down the centre of either side of the cut. The ridge should run from the point of the cone to its wide base.

8 ✳ Remove the knife and allow to dry.

Leaves

1 ✽ Press a real leaf into thinly rolled-out modelling paste, then cut out the shape.

2 ✽ When it is dry, paint it with a mixture of leaf-green and yellow food colouring straight from the bottle.

Assembly

To use as a spray on its own, make vine stems by rolling some modelling paste thinly, then colouring it the same as the leaves. Arrange and place the leaves in groups with the buds and scattered flowers. If you are using it as a filler, 2 flowers, 1 bud and 2 leaves are sufficient.

AZALEA

This is a very useful flower for cake decorations. It is relatively easy to make and comes in many different colours, including white with a rim of colour around the petals. Four of the petals are the same size, the fifth is slightly wider. I form and dry these in a cup of aluminium (aluminum) foil held in a Plasticine holder (see p 51).

Method

1 ✽ Use white or pale-coloured modelling paste. Make a bean 2½ cm (1 in) long, rounded at the top and pointed at the bottom.

2 ✽ Flatten and thin the petal out finely. Gently round the top into a point by easing it between your fingers.

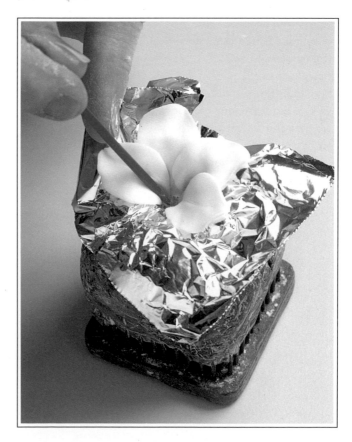

3 ✽ Place the petal in the Plasticine holder and ease it backwards with a ball tool.

4 ✠ Make the second petal and place it next to the first one, just overlapping at the bottom.

5 ✠ Make another 2 petals. Mark them down the centre with the back of a knife to cup them a little.

6 ✠ Place these 2 petals into the holder, one facing 3 o'clock and the other facing 9 o'clock. The pointed ends should be inserted down into the holder.

7 ✠ Make the fifth petal wider. Mark down the centre with a ball tool.

8 ✠ Place it in the holder, facing 6 o'clock, with its tail covering the tails of the other petals in the throat of the flower.

9 ✠ Take the flower, still in the aluminium foil, out of the holder. Gently squeeze the back of the flower to close up its centre around the straight end of a ball tool. Leave just enough space for a small dot of royal icing to hold the stamens in place. Allow to dry.

10 ✠ If you have used white modelling paste, paint the entire flower with food colouring mixed with pure alcohol. Allow to dry thoroughly before painting the dots of colour in the throat. Give the flower coloured paste, you will only need to paint in the dots of colour.

11 ✠ When the flower is dry, use a dot of royal icing to fix the stamens in the throat of the flower. You will need 5 stamens with small heads and a larger one with a large head. The colour of the stamens should match the flower.

PRIMROSE

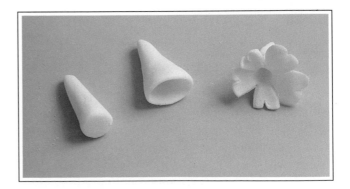

Each of the 5 pale yellow petals have a cleft in the centre and a tiny orange triangle at the base pointing towards the centre. This triangle makes the 'eye' of the flower.

Method

1 ✧ Hollow out a 3 cm (1¼ in) long cone of white modelling paste to one-third of the way down. Make the rim about 1¼ cm (½ in) diameter.

2 ✧ Make 5 short cuts around the rim to create 5 equal-sized petals. Open the flower out a little.

3 ✧ Round the petal corners and make a shallow cut in the centre of the top of each one. Flatten out each petal to make it heart-shaped.

4 ✧ Wire the bell. Do not smooth the paste down on the wire.

5 ✧ Turn the flower upside down and make 3 snips into the paste about halfway down the bell. Ease the snipped paste out and shape to make a calyx. Firm it onto the wire.

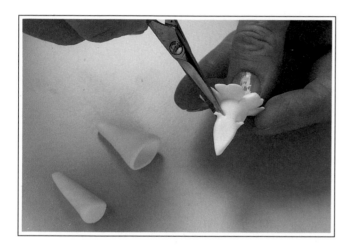

6 ✧ Mix egg-yellow food colouring, plus a touch of orange and lemon-yellow food colouring, with pure alcohol. Paint the back of the flower, then the front. Leave to dry.

7 ✧ When thoroughly dry, paint a tiny orange triangle across the base of each petal. The point of the triangle should face into the centre, and should be no more than one-quarter the length of the petal.

8 ✧ Paint the calyx pale green.

9 ✧ Put a very small dob of royal icing deep into the throat of the flower. Insert 4–5 cream-coloured stamens.

PANSY

Making this pretty flower is reasonably easy, but colouring it is not. It is a good idea to study the real flower. The 5 petals can be made and dried separately or made and placed into the dry calyx when still wet. I prefer to make them separately, then assemble them. The petals are arranged in 2 pairs with 1 base petal. The petals are in the shape of a Dainty Bess petal, and range from 2 cm (¾ in) to 2½ cm (1 in) in size.

Flower

1 ✧ For the 2 top petals, make 2 Dainty Bess petals (see p 35). Cut and flute them slightly and dry flat with their points just overlapping.

2 ✧ Make the 2 side petals the same shape. When cupping them in the palm of your hand, place the point facing across the palm. Flute slightly, and dry flat.

3 ✳ Make the base petal in a Dainty Bess shape, but pull both sides out wider, leaving the point in the centre. Cup and flute. Dry flat.

4 ✳ The point of each petal forms the centre face of the pansy.

Colouring

1 ✳ Using food colouring, wash all the petals in a basic pale colour and allow to dry thoroughly.
2 ✳ Use the palest colour furthest from the centre. The idea is to have the shades of colour deepen as you reach the centre point.
3 ✳ When you paint a darker colour onto the petal, wash the brush and dry it until it is damp, not wet. Using the brush in a push–pull movement, smudge the 2 colours together where they meet.
4 ✳ Each colour that you add must shade and smudge into the one before. Do not leave defined edges between colours.
5 ✳ If you use black to darken the centre area, be careful. I find it's better to use the non-toxic felt pens.

Assembly

1 ✳ Place a dob of royal icing onto a square of waxed paper.
2 ✳ Place the points of the top 2 petals, just overlapping, in the royal icing.
3 ✳ Place the 2 side petals in the royal icing, their points touching at the centre.
4 ✳ Place the base petal in the icing. Make sure its point fits up into the small space left between the 2 side ones.
5 ✳ When dry, pipe a very tiny horseshoe of royal icing in the centre to cover the points of the 5 petals. When this is dry, paint a soft yellow.

6 ✳ Attach a wet, wired calyx to the dry, assembled flower.

Leaves

1 ✳ Make a long, flat shape, with rounded indentations.
2 ✳ Paint a lightish leaf-green colour.

CATTLEYA ORCHID

Orchids are heavy flowers and must be made well. The cattleya orchid is one of the softer ones and looks very pleasing so long as the fluting of the 2 wing petals and the lip is well done, and the paste is as fine as possible. They are usually used as the main flower and are suitable for any kind of cake. If they are to be the theme of a wedding cake, use 2 on the bottom tier and 3 on the top tier. Soften with fillers and tulle.

Flower

petal. It should run the full length up to the point of the petal. Flute the edges with a round toothpick (wooden pick).

1 ✳ Make 3 long finger-shaped sepals, about 5 cm (2 in) in length in white modelling paste. Curve them backwards. Allow to dry.

3 ✳ While wet, turn the petal over. Hold it in the palm of your left hand and run a ball tool (see p 5) up and down both sides of the central vein. This will cup out the front of the petals.

2 ✳ Make 2 wing petals in the shape of a large Dainty Bess petal, but longer. With the back of a knife, mark a central vein along the back of the

4 ✻ Turn the petal back over. It should have a slightly backward curve. Dry.

Lip

1 ✻ Hollow out a 2½ cm (1 in) long cone of white modelling paste. Extend the bottom half of the cone by gently pulling down.
2 ✻ Cut the top edge into 2 halves and round the cut edges.
3 ✻ Make the lower half of the cone very fine with your fingers. Cut a 1 cm (½ in) V-shape into this lower edge. Slightly round the corners of the 'V'.
4 ✻ Flute with a round toothpick around both edges of the 'V' from the top cut to the bottom. Make them as fluted as possible.
5 ✻ Reshape the throat of the lip with a No 3 former too. Dry, allowing the lower edge to come to the front.

Colouring

1 ✻ Spray the 3 sepals and the 2 wing petals with a soft pink food colouring mixed with pure alcohol. Allow to dry.
2 ✻ Apply yellow chalk to the throat of the lip, bringing the colour out about halfway. Brush a dark pink chalk over the rest of the lip, from where the yellow ends right out to the edges.
3 ✻ Dust around the edges of the 2 wing petal with a darker pink.

This species comes in many colours. For example, the flower can be left white with just a yellow-throated lip.

Assembly

1 ✻ Put a drop of royal icing on a square of waxed paper.
2 ✻ Place the lip in the centre with a front sepal on either side. Allow this to set for about 2 minutes.
3 ✻ Place the wing petals behind and to the side of the front sepals. Support them from behind with cottonwool balls and allow to set for 2 minutes.
4 ✻ Set in the back sepal, which is placed standing up in the centre.
5 ✻ Support the entire flower with waxed paper and leave to dry.

CLEMATIS

This flower fascinates me because of the softness of its colourings and the starkness of its black eye and black stamens. There are 8 petals, all the same size and shape. They are only slightly curved, and I find a curved patty tin (pan) excellent for drying them in.

Method

1 ✻ Mould a 2½ cm (1 in) long bean in white modelling paste with a point at both ends. Flatten then widen the middle section.
2 ✻ Gently roll out as thin as possible.
3 ✻ Cut into an oval leaf shape, keeping a very thin point at the top end.

4 ✤ Mark with the back of a knife from the bottom point to halfway up the centre of the petal. Make more marks that fan out on either side of this central mark, shortening them as you near the edges.

5 ✤ Press the front side of the petal into a pad of crepe paper to give it texture.

6 ✤ Gently flute at one point on either side of the top half of the petal.

7 ✤ Dry in a patty tin (pan).

8 ✤ Make 8 petals for each flower.

9 ✤ When completely dry, paint the back of the petal, then the front, with a pale food colouring mixed with pure alcohol. Allow to dry. Some of these flowers have a darker splash of colour up the centre of each petal, which you can add if you wish.

Assembly

The petals fit together in an unusual way, so I use the clock face as a guide to their position. Place a small amount of royal icing on a square of waxed paper and position the petals in this order:

    petal 1 at 2 o'clock

    petal 2 at 10 o'clock

    petal 3 at 5 o'clock

    petal 4 at 7 o'clock

    petal 5 at 3 o'clock

    petal 6 at 9 o'clock

    petal 7 under petals 3 and 4

    petal 8 on top of petals 1 and 2, at 12 o'clock.

With a clean brush, work the remaining royal icing up to a raised central peak. Leave enough icing around the peak for short pieces of black cotton, which form the stamens. When this is dry, paint the area of royal icing around the cotton a pale yellow. Paint the peak black and leave the tiniest white spot in the centre.

QUICK AND EASY ORCHID

If you have a cake that has to be decorated quickly, a flower that will cover a good-sized area is very handy. With this in mind, I created this orchid. The petals are cut with the middle-sized frangipani cutter, and I use a little mint lady for the lip. If it is not big enough, a larger cutter can be used and the lip made from a mint lady that is also slightly larger. The colouring is taken from the cattleya orchid.

Method

1 ✱ Cut 5 petals with the frangipani cutter. Trim the rounded end to a point on 4 of the petals.
2 ✱ With a knife, make 5 markings, in a fan shape, from the point to halfway up the petal.
3 ✱ Twist 2 petals slightly and dry flat (the side petals).
4 ✱ Curve 2 petals into a crescent and set them on their side to dry (the upper side petals).

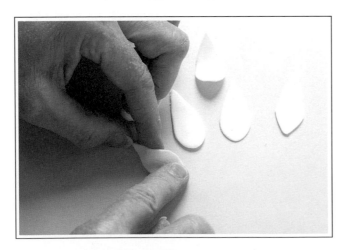

5 ✱ Shape the rounded fifth petal into a crescent and set on its side to dry (the centre back petal). This petal must fill a wider space than the others.
6 ✱ Make a little peppermint lady for the lip (see p 54), but do not cut the bottom section into 3 segments. Leave in one piece and roll well with a round toothpick (wooden pick). Re-cup the throat with a No 2 former tool and allow to dry.

Colouring

1 ✱ Colour the base of each petal with yellow food colouring mixed with pure alcohol. When half-dry, paint the back then the front with peach food colouring mixed with pure alcohol, taking in the edge of the yellow.
2 ✱ When dry, dust rust-coloured chalk lightly up the centre of each petal.
3 ✱ Colour the throat of the lip with yellow chalk. Paint the back and front of the lip with lemon-yellow food colouring straight from the bottle. When dry, dust the edge of the lip with a deeper pink chalk — make this edging of colour about 3 mm (⅛ in) wide.

Assembly

Put a dot of royal icing on a square of waxed paper. Set the 2 side petals into the icing facing the front, leaving enough room for the lip. Set the lip in place. Leave to dry. Place the 2 upper side petals in the icing and support them from the back with a cottonwool ball. Allow to set a little. Put a small amount of royal icing at the back of the throat and set in the back centre petal. Support it with cotton-wool balls until it is dry and firm.

JAPONICA

The first of the spring flowers, the flowering quince, as the japonica is commonly known, has flowers of glowing red which contrast beautifully with the dark green leaves. It makes a lovely decoration for a fortieth (ruby) wedding anniversary cake.

Calyx

1 ✠ Hollow out a 1 cm (½ in) long cone of white modelling paste and make 5 cuts in the rim to form equal-sized sepals.

2 ✠ Mitre the sepals to a long point. Flatten and slightly cup each one.

3 ✠ Attach to a hooked wire and allow to dry.

4 ✠ Paint dark green.

Flower

1 ✠ Make 5 Dainty Bess petals (see p 35) in white modelling paste about 2 cm (¾ in) in size. Cup each one slightly, gently flute the top edge and leave to dry.

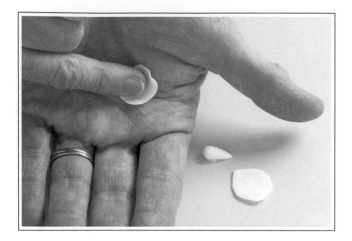

Leaves

1 ✺ Roll a bean of paste about 1 cm (½ in) long and push a single wire right up into the middle. Flatten as finely as possible.

2 ✺ Paint the back and front of the petals with scarlet and a touch of orange food colouring. The colours can be used straight from the bottle.

3 ✺ Using a little royal icing to hold them in place, put the 5 dry and painted petals into the dry calyx so that each one just overlaps the preceding one at the point.

4 ✺ Fill the centre of the flower with tiny yellow stamen threads. When they have set in the royal icing, tip each one with brown food colouring.

Buds

Make a medium-sized bud. Paint it red, then paint on a dark green calyx. The wires holding the flowers and the buds should be painted the same green as the calyx.

2 ✺ Cut in the shape of a rose leaf, serrate the edges and mark in the veins.

3 ✺ Bend the wire slightly in the leaf. Allow to dry and paint in the same dark green as the calyx.

Wildflowers

KURRAJONG

The flowers of this native tree are either red and white, yellow and orange, or white with red spots. The strong colours make them very useful as decorations for a cake made for a man.

Flower

1 ✽ Hollow out a 1¼ cm (½ in) long cone of white modelling paste with a hair-roller pin. Widen the rim.

2 ✽ Make 5 short cuts, equally spaced apart, around the rim.

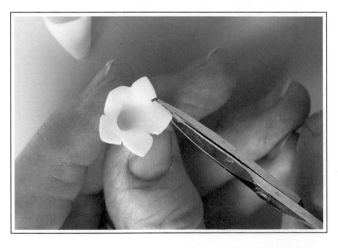

3 ✽ Neatly mitre the top of the petals and flatten them gently.

4 ✽ Use a ball tool to open up the base of the flower and make a shallow bell.

5 ✽ Insert a knotted wire.

6 ✽ Turn the flower over and, using a ball tool, ball (see p 5) each petal from the back.

7 ✽ Turn the flower right-side up and arrange the petals so that they stand out at a 90° angle from the rim.

8 ✽ Paint the back of the flower with scarlet or pillar-box red food colouring straight from the bottle. Do not let the colour touch the front edges of the petals. Allow to dry.

9 ✽ Mix some red and orange chalk. Paint the throat of the flower from the bottom up to where the bell shape begins.

10 ✽ Insert 2–3 red or yellow stamens with a dot of royal icing to secure them.

Note
If you are making a white flower, you will only need to paint red dots on the back of the bell, and a deeper yellow on the throat.

Buds

1 ✽ Wrap a piece of paste about two-thirds the length of the flower around the hooked end of a piece of wire. Firm it into place.

2 ✽ Shape the head to make it bulbous. Mark it to show 5 closed petals.

3 ✽ Paint the bud red, leaving a little white at the tip.

BORONIA

There are many varieties of boronia. I find the brown and the pink varieties the easiest to make — their colours blend beautifully in wildflower arrangements.

Brown Boronia

1 ✵ Hollow out a ½ cm (¼ in) long cone of yellow modelling paste.

2 ✵ Make 4 short cuts an equal distance apart around the rim to create 4 petals.

3 ✵ Round the top of each petal and use a small ball tool (see p 5) to cup each petal gently.

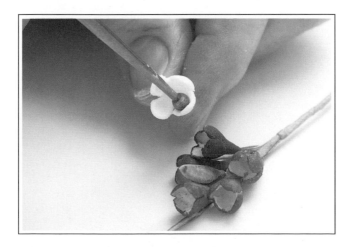

4 ✵ Insert a knotted wire into the flower.

5 ✵ Work the ball tool in the centre of the flower to bring all 4 petals up to form a cup. Allow to dry.

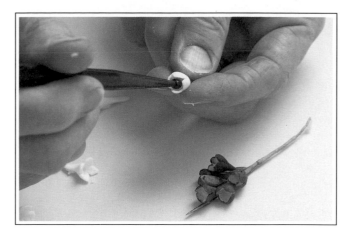

6 ✵ Paint the outside of the flower chestnut-brown with food colouring straight from the bottle. Do not forget the edges.

PINK BORONIA

1 ✵ Hollow out a 1 cm (½ in) long cone of pale burgundy-pink modelling paste.

2 ✵ Make 4 or 5 short cuts an equal distance apart around the rim of the cone. Some flowers can have 4 petals, some 5.

3 ✳ Mitre each petal to a soft point and flatten gently.

4 ✳ Wire the flower and re-form the centre, cupping it a little. Allow to dry.

5 ✳ If you wish, you can insert one dark stamen. Hold it in place with a tiny dot of royal icing.

6 ✳ Paint the back of the flower with burgundy-pink food colouring straight from the bottle. Do not forget the edges.

Buds

Brown boronia buds are short and bulbous. Pink boronia buds are long, thin and pointed.

Assembly

A small spray is made with 3 flowers and a bud.

CHRISTMAS BELLS

These beautiful flowers have details that I didn't notice for many years — for instance, the tiny speck of green on the tip of each petal. I suggest you study the real flower or a good photograph of one.

Flower

1 ✳ Make a cone of pale yellow modelling paste approximately two-thirds the size of the finished flower.

2 ✳ Hollow out the centre of the cone using a hair-roller pin. Roll the cone gently twice, then ease the pin into the cone and use it to lengthen the cone into a bell shape of the required depth. Do not let the cone spread outwards too much.

3 ✳ Make short cuts around the rim to divide it into halves.

4 ✳ Make 3 short cuts within each half. You now have 6 petals of equal size.

5 ✳ Curve the petals.

6 ✳ Working from the inside, gently roll each petal with the hair-roller pin, making sure the pin is well down inside the bell. This will curve the petals and at the same time reshape the bell.

7 ✤ Insert the rounded end of the pin well down into the bell.

8 ✤ Insert a wire with a knotted end into the flower. Allow to dry.

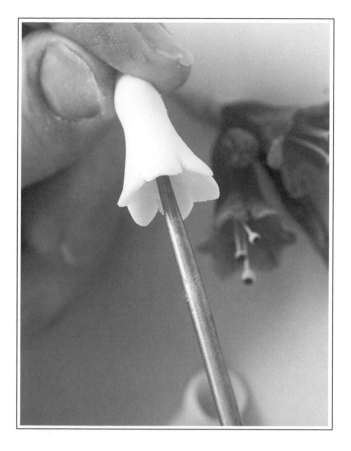

Colouring

1 ✤ Mix a little orange food colouring with water and paint the inside and outside of the bell.

2 ✤ While the colour is still damp but not wet, dab a spot of scarlet or pillar-box red food colouring on the outside of the flower at the rounded end of the

bell. Gently smudge this down towards the wide part of the bell. Leave a margin of orange about 3 mm (⅛ in) wide from the edge of the petals. The colours must merge without any hard edges.

3 ✤ Paint a tiny speck of green on each petal and a pale green calyx at the wired end of the bell.

Leaves

Shape a small bean of paste into a long, thin leaf that is smooth and slightly curved.

Assembly

To make a spray, use 3 flowers with a bud.

WARATAH

There are 2 ways to make these flowers. One is very quick and easy, and the other takes time and effort, but produces a much better looking flower. If the flower is needed for the side of a small cake, use the quick method. But if the spray is going to be the main theme on the top of a cake or plaque, more detail and greater care are needed. Always use modelling paste coloured with pillar-box red food colouring powder, and make sure it is worked through the paste well. To make this flower in white paste then paint it afterwards is a waste of time and an unnecessary test of patience.

Method 1 — Quick and Easy

1 ✤ Take a ball of red paste about 3½ cm (1½ in) in size. Make sure it is smooth. Cover it with a square of large-holed nylon net.

2 ✤ Gather the net around the ball and twist it so tight that the paste is pushed through the holes in the net.

3 ✤ Squeeze until the tracts in the paste are long enough. (Don't squeeze so hard that the paste falls out through the net.)

4 ✤ Tighten the net under the ball and cut off the excess.

5 ✤ Set the ball down carefully and allow to dry.

6 ✤ Make about 10 leaf-shaped outer petals.

7 ✤ Arrange the first row of 5 petals around the ball. They should curve up around the centre.

8 ✤ Place the outer row standing away from the inner row. Make sure that they do not make the flower look like a starfish. Some should be cupped slightly upwards.

Method 2 — Time and Effort

1 ✤ Working with red paste, make about 20 comma-shaped pieces in 6 different sizes. To do this, roll a small piece of paste between your fingers, leaving 1 end with a head and the other end with a sharp point. Curve them around your fingertip to form the comma shape.

2 ✤ Lay out in rows to dry. Make the last 2 rows with longer tails.

3 ✤ When their tails are dry, make a tiny petal. Wrap it around the comma from the inside curve to the outside.

4 ✤ Allow the commas and petals to dry thoroughly. Keep the longer tailed commas with petals attached to one side.

5 ✤ Take a ball of red fondant about 3½ cm (1½ in) in size. Pierce 3 holes in the base to allow it to dry without splitting.

6 ✤ Shape into a blunt-ended dome, slightly tapered at both ends.

7 ✤ Start at the top of the dome. Push the pointed end of the commas into the damp fondant, allowing the curve to nestle onto the ball. Make sure this first circle of commas covers the top of the ball.

8 ✤ Work your way down the cone. Place the commas between or close up to the ones above.

9 ✤ For the last row at the base of the cone, use the longer tailed commas with the little petals.

10 ✤ Push a round toothpick (wooden pick) up into the base of the ball. This will form a stem to make handling easier when the paste has dried.

11 ✤ To dry, place a square of waxed paper into the concave area of a wooden drying rack. Pass the toothpick through one of the holes in the rack and allow the flower to nestle in the concave area and dry.

12 ✤ Make leaf-shaped red petals as fine as possible. Take a bean 1¼ cm (½ in) long and spread it out using your fingers. Keep a point at one end. Extend this until it is very fine and pinch gently. Widen the petal in the middle and leave a blunt end at the other end.

13 ✵ Now place a hair-roller pin down the length of the petal and gently roll it from side to side. The petal will curve up slightly.

14 ✵ Place an inner row of these petals up around the base of the centre so that they curve onto the commas.

15 ✵ Stand the second row of petals out from the first. Make sure they do not give the flower a starfish look.

The toothpick can be used to set the flower onto the side of the cake. However, it's best to cut it off if the flower is to be set flat.

WEDGE PEA

I couldn't resist the colours of this flower, a relative of the sweet pea. The size and shape of the flowers are much the same, but the front crescent is placed differently.

Method

1 ✵ Make a ½ cm (¼ in) long crescent of white modelling paste. Insert the hooked end of a piece of wire into it.

2 ✵ Make a Dainty Bess petal about 1½ cm (¾ in) in size. Hollow it out slightly from the back.

3 ✵ Moisten the petal and attach to the back of the crescent. Make sure the petal stands up well.

4 ✵ Curve the end of the crescent forwards and slightly downwards, leaving the petal standing up and away from it.

5 ✵ Colour the crescent and the lower half of the petal with lipstick-pink powdered chalk.

6 ✵ Colour the rest of the petal with yellow chalk.

7 ✵ Colour the edges of the petal with the pink chalk.

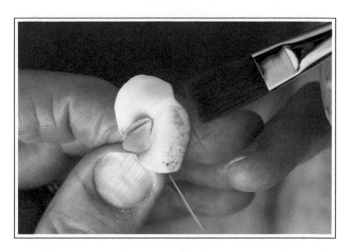

8 ✵ Roll 2 very tiny balls of paste. Moisten and attach one on either side of the crescent, near the bottom at the front. Allow to dry. Colour them a bright yellow — they should look like two small eyes.

STURT'S DESERT PEA

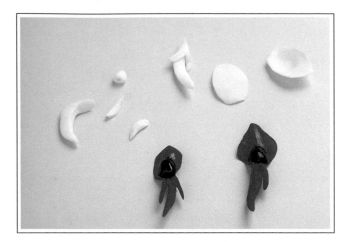

This striking flower adds that extra something to a spray of native flowers. Be careful to keep the size in proportion to the other flowers in the spray.

Method

1 ✳ Make a crescent-shaped petal approximately 2½ cm (1 in) long from white modelling paste and curve the tail forwards and upwards.

2 ✳ Make two small teardrops of paste ½ cm (¼ in) long. Fold the long edges towards each other to form an ear.

3 ✳ Moisten and attach on either side of the front of the crescent at the top.

4 ✳ Shape the ends of all 3 petals together to a point. Allow to dry.

5 ✳ Make a small ball of paste and attach it to the point with a dab of glue (made from modelling paste dissolved in water until it becomes mushy).

6 ✳ If you decide to wire the flower, insert the hooked wire into the ball now. Allow to dry.

7 ✳ Make a petal from a small triangle of paste, with a rounded base.

8 ✳ Flute the straight edges.

9 ✳ Place the petal in the palm of your hand and hollow out the centre of the rounded base.

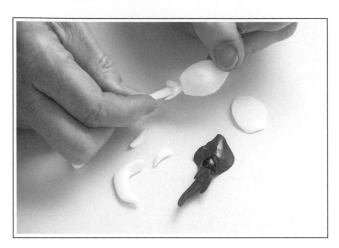

10 ✳ Lightly wet the underside of the petal and place it across the top of the 3 joined petals at the point where the ball is attached. Quickly lift it up towards, over and around the ball to make a bulge. Ease the rest of the petal backwards so that it stands up well. Look at photographs of the flower to see exactly how to shape this bulge. Allow to dry.

Colouring

1 ✳ Paint the entire flower except for the bulge with scarlet food colouring. Bring the colour to the edges of the petals and close to the underside of the bulge. Allow to dry.

2 ✳ Mix a little black and violet food colouring and paint the bulge, feathering the colour out into the scarlet.

GUMNUTS

The light brown colour of gumnuts looks very effective in a spray of native flowers.

Method

1 ✽ Make a small dumpy cone of nut-brown modelling paste. Open it up with a small ball tool until it is as wide across the top of the cone as it is long. Wire and allow to dry.

2 ✽ Roll out a small piece of paste to fill the hollow in the cone. Dampen it and fit it into place. Make a cross on its flat top.

3 ✽ Paint some gumnuts a darker brown and some green.

GUM BLOSSOM

These unusual flowers are made from threads of brightly coloured red, orange or yellow cotton sewing thread set in dark brown or dark green gumnuts. They soften a spray of other native flowers.

Flower

1 ✽ Hold the thumb and forefinger of one hand 1¼ cm (½ in) apart and, leaving a tail of cotton hanging, wind cotton sewing thread around them 20 times.

2 ✽ Take the thread off your fingers. Tie the tail around the centre of the loop to make a figure 8 and tie off. Bind the centre of the loop with fine wire, leaving a long end.

3 ✽ Fold the figure 8 of thread in half so that all the loops face in the same direction. Bind the wire around it so that all the loops are standing up at the end of the wire stem.

4 ✽ Cut the top of the loops open.

5 ✻ Make a gumnut from brown or green modelling paste. Pass the bottom of the wire through it and push the gumnut up to fit neatly around the flower. Neaten onto the wire. Leave to dry.

6 ✻ Separate the threads. Touch the tips lightly with a little glue (made by dissolving scraps of modelling paste in water till they become mushy). Dip the threads in some powdered gelatin mixed with either green or yellow powdered chalk. Only a speck on each thread is needed. Do not make the tips lumpy.

Leaves

The leaf is long and thin, tapering to a point at the top, with one central vein.

Assembly

Use 3 flowers and 3 leaves to make a spray.

TEA-TREE

The pretty mauve-pink colour of the flowers and the dark green of the leaves makes the tea-tree very useful as a filler for a spray of native flowers.

Flower

1 ✻ Hollow out a small cone of white modelling paste with a round toothpick (wooden pick).
2 ✻ Make 5 short cuts in the rim to create 5 petals.
3 ✻ Gently smooth away the curves of each petal.
4 ✻ Flatten each petal, pushing the paste sideways.
5 ✻ Indent the centre with the small ball tool. Allow to dry.
6 ✻ Mix burgundy-pink and mauve-pink food colouring with pure alcohol. Paint the back of the petals, then paint the front. Allow to dry.

7 ✽ Fill the hollow centre of the flower with royal icing. Bring it up to a peak. Allow to dry.

8 ✽ Paint the centre a blackish-green.

Leaves

1 ✽ Neaten a long bean of paste onto a knotted wire and flatten to make a long, spindly leaf.

2 ✽ Paint dark green.

FLANNEL FLOWER

This is certainly one of the prettiest native flowers, but also one of the hardest to make. I have tried many ways — cutting it like a daisy, working on a ring, making it petal by petal and assembling when dry. I have found that the best method is to make and dry the centre, then place the wet petals onto it. You must work very quickly, however, and of course, work in white paste.

Centre

1 ✽ Wire a ball of fondant about 1¼ cm (½ in) in size — any bigger and the flower will be out of proportion to the waratah, which it usually accompanies in a spray. Allow to dry.

2 ✽ Mix together some dry powdered gelatin and finely dusted moss-green chalk. Place in a container.

3 ✽ Paint the top half of the dried centre with green colouring and dip it into the dry mixture while still damp. Allow to dry.

Flower

1 ✽ Make 5 or 6 finely pointed petals that widen in the middle and narrow towards the bottom.

2 ✽ Fit the damp petals around the centre and make firm.

3 ✽ Make another 4 or 5 petals and fit these behind the first row, filling in the spaces. Allow to dry.

4 ✽ Paint the back of the petal with pale yellow food colouring mixed with pure alcohol.

5 ✽ Touch the tip of each petal with glue (made by dissolving a few scraps of modelling paste in water until they become mushy). Dip them in the gelatin and chalk mixture used for the centre.

GERALDTON WAX AND ESPERANCE

Both these flowers take their names from the areas in which they grow in Western Australia. They make very effective fillers for a spray of native flowers. Geraldton wax is pink with deeper pink centre. Esperance is snow-white with a sharp, lime-green centre.

Method

1 ✤ Hollow out a 1¼ cm (½ in) cone of white modelling paste with a round toothpick (wooden pick).
2 ✤ Make 5 short cuts in the rim to create 5 petals.
3 ✤ Trim the corners of each petal very slightly.

4 ✤ Place the open blades of your scissors either side of the base of the petal and squeeze gently.

5 ✤ Flatten each petal, then cup using a small ball tool.

6 ✤ Indent the centre of each petal with the ball tool. Cut away the paste at the back of the flower so that it can dry flat.
7 ✤ Wire a very small gumnut shape. Fill it with royal icing and set the flower in it. Allow to dry.
8 ✤ Use a very fine pipe to pipe a dot of royal icing at the base of each petal, on the edge of the indented centre. Pipe a long, pulled dot in the centre of it.

Colouring

1 ✤ Mix pink-mauve food colouring with pure alcohol. Paint the back of the Geraldton wax flower. When dry, paint the centre in a darker shade of the same colour.
2 ✤ Esperance is pure white. Paint the centre a sharp lime-green (moss-green with a touch of yellow). Pull up a dot of lime-green royal icing at the base of each petal around the indented area.

CHRISTMAS BUSH

The pink 'flowers' left on the bush when the white flowers have finished are actually the calyx. They enlarge and gradually turn the colour that gives the bush its name. As it is not a true red, you will have to mix the colours carefully.

Flower

1 ✤ Hollow out a tiny cone of white modelling paste with a round toothpick (wooden pick).

2 ❁ Make 5 long cuts of equal depth, equally spaced apart, to create 5 petals.

3 ❁ Mitre each petal, cupping the centre very slightly.

4 ❁ Flatten and shape upwards.

5 ❁ Wire the flower, re-cupping the centre and neatening the back onto the wire. Make some flowers with half-closed petals to give variety.

6 ❁ Paint the centre of the flower yellow. Allow to dry.

7 ❁ Mix rose-pink food colouring and a touch of orange food colouring with pure alcohol. Paint the back of the petals. Paint the front of the petals. Work from the middle of the flower outwards, leaving a small margin of white around the yellow centre.

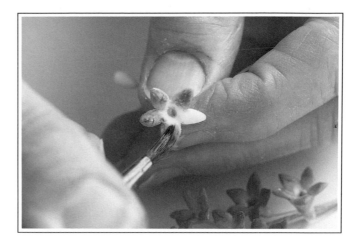

Buds

1 ❁ Shape a small piece of white modelling paste onto the end of a knotted piece of wire to make a long, slender bud.

2 ❁ Paint the bud pink with a little yellow showing at the tip.

Leaves

The leaves are made up of small leaflets with finely serrated edges, rather like a miniature maple leaf. Paint them a light emerald-green with a touch of yellow.

Assembly

Assemble 5 flowers and 4 buds to make a cluster for use as a filler. Wire each flower and bud separately and bind the wires together with pale green tissue paper or Stemtex. Do not use Parafilm — it is too heavy.

Decorating Sides

EXTENSION

A skirt border decoration around the base of a cake, consisting of finely piped threads of royal icing extending to a scalloped edge along the bottom, is called 'extension'. It is also referred to as 'bridgework', 'dropwork', or 'threadwork'. The scalloped edge is the extension and the threadwork of the skirt is the bridgework or dropwork.

If you are a beginner, develop your skills by practising on the side of a cake tin (pan) before working on a cake.

1 ✱ Measure the length and height of one side of the cake and cut a piece of greaseproof paper to this size for a template. (If it is a round cake, cut the paper long enough to encircle the cake.)

2 ✱ Fold the paper in half crossways. Cut a half-scallop at both ends of the template. The half-

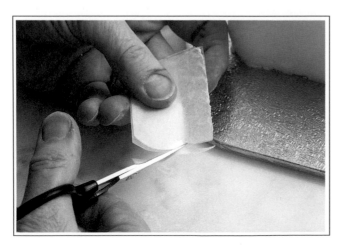

scallop at the corner of the cake will meet the half-scallop from the adjoining side. This avoids an ugly finish at each corner of the cake.

3 ✱ With the template folded in half, fold again up to the beginning of the half-scallop and continue until the desired scallop size is obtained. Cut a shallow curve through all thicknesses of the template to create the scallop pattern. When you open the template, there will be a half-scallop at both ends.

4 ✱ Fold the template in half crossways, then fold lengthways to form the top design of the extension. The fold can be a straight line 3 cm (1¼ in) above the scallop line, or the line can be lower at either end and meet at a central point 3 cm (1¼ in) above the scallop line. You can use any variation that pleases you. This line marks the position from which the threadwork drops down to the extended scallops.

5 ✱ Pipe a small snail's trail around the base of the cake to neaten the bottom edge and to fasten the cake to the board.

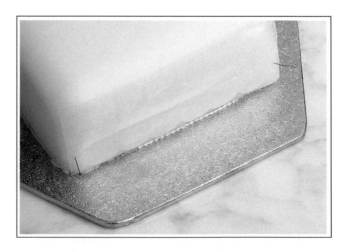

6 ✱ Pin both ends of the template onto the side of the cake, making sure that the scallops just touch the snail's trail. If the scallops are any lower, they will fasten onto the board and break when the cake is moved. On the other hand, if the edge is too high, the skirt will not cover the bottom neatly.

7 ✱ Using the blunt end of a 3¼ mm (No 10 (UK/Canada), No 3 (US)) knitting needle, trace the design over the paper template onto the cake. Repeat on all sides, being sure to match up the corner scallops.

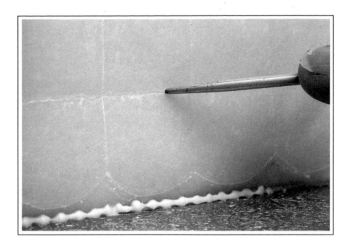

8 ✠ Using a size 2 tube, pipe a row of royal icing over the scallop design. When the row is thoroughly dry, pipe another row over the first. Repeat this 6 times. Make sure each row covers the one before evenly and that it touches at all points.

9 ✠ After the extension is dry (it may take a few hours), use a size 00 tube and a new batch of royal icing to attach the threadwork. Hold the tube firmly and use even pressure. Start from the top line of the design and draw the thread down and out onto the built-out scallop design. Continue to add the threadwork, being careful to watch that:
• the space between each thread is close and equal
• the tension of each thread is the same.

CUTTER DESIGNS

Commercial cutters are available in numerous designs. They can be used individually or to build a design using fondant. In the photograph I have used flower cutters.

1 ✠ Roll out a 3 mm (⅛ in) thick sheet of fondant. Cut out a flower and remove the 2 lower petals.
2 ✠ Use a small daisy cutter to remove the centre from the flower.

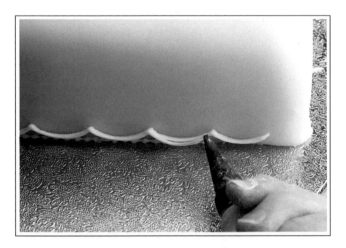

10 ✠ Once the threadwork is dry, finish the bottom edge with scallops, tiny loops, a fine rope design or dots. The top edge can be finished by applying lace pieces or tiny loops and dots.

3 ✠ Curve the design into a shallow 'U' shape and allow to dry.
4 ✠ Attach to the side of the cake with royal icing. Some designs, when attached over a ribbon, allow the ribbon to show through the central cut-out.

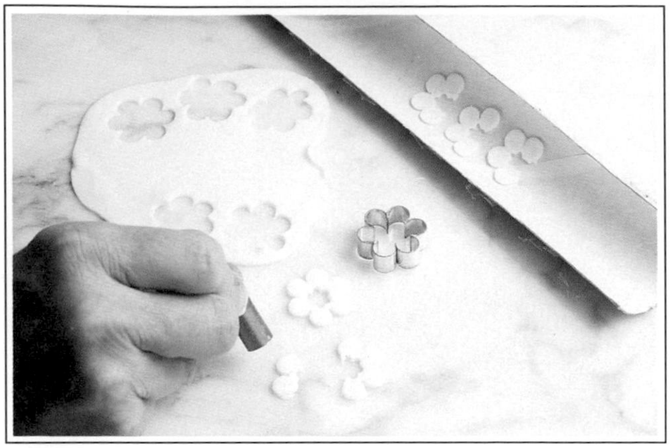

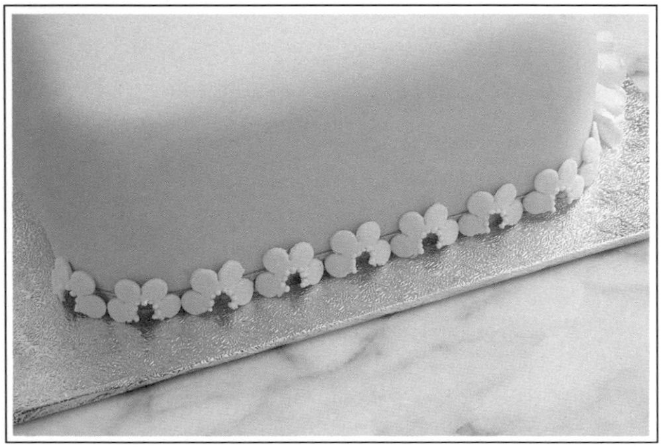

FRILL

The original frill is the Garrett Frill from South Africa. It can be placed around the cake or up over the sides of the cake. A Garrett Frill cutter enables you to make this decoration easily.

1 ❋ Roll fondant out to 3 mm (⅛ in) thick. Cut with the Garrett Frill cutter.

2 ❋ Cut the design in half. Press with a rounded toothpick (wooden pick) and fan out each scallop until it starts to frill.

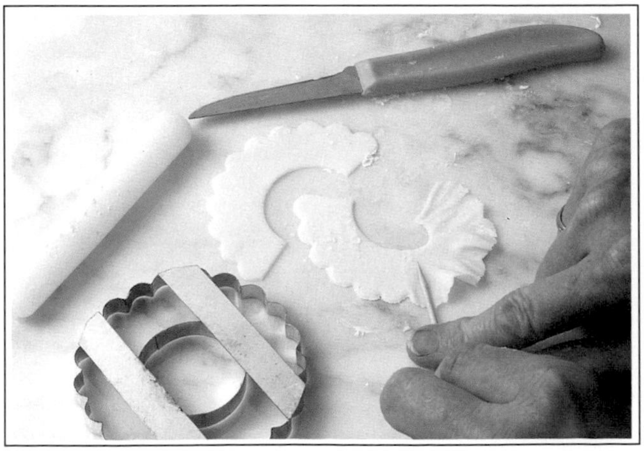

3 ❋ Trim the top edge to an even width. Attach to the cake with egg white or water.

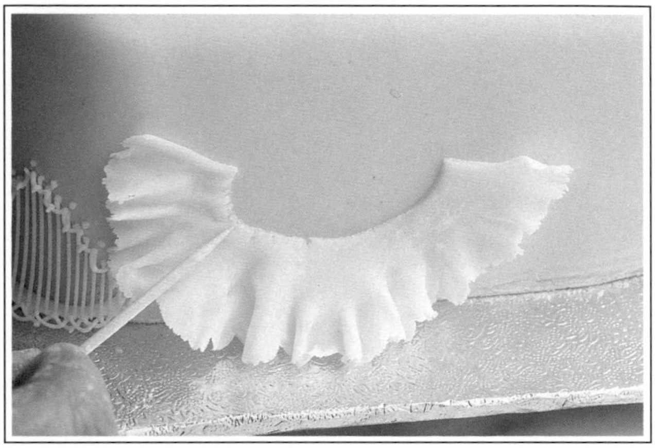

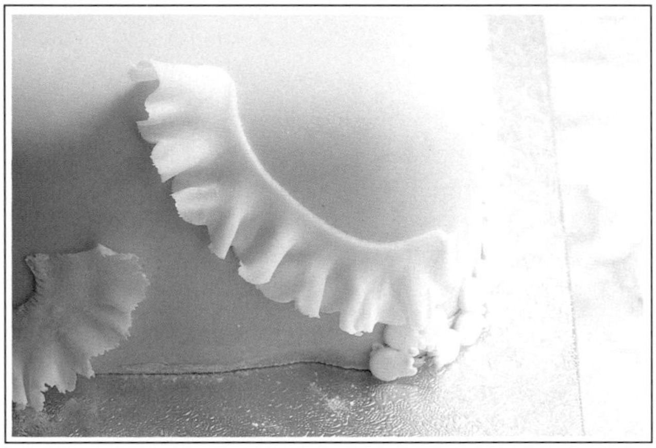

4 ❋ Finish the top with a lace edging or the imprint of a smaller cutter.

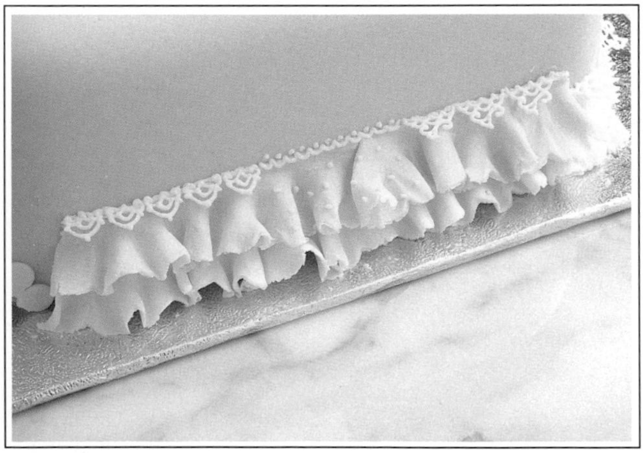

Marzipan Fruit

make apples, pears, strawberries, bananas, cherries, oranges, grapes etc, to give a good assortment of colours.

Simply mould the fruit to the appropriate shape from a small ball of marzipan. Place a clove in the top for the stalk, and another in the bottom. Leave to dry. Paint when the paste is firm with food colouring either used straight from the bottle or diluted with water. You can make vegetables in the same way.

FRUIT BARRELS

I make fruit barrels in which to present the marzipan fruit. The top of a Tupperware eggcup is the perfect size for a mould.

Marzipan fruits are made from the almond paste used to cover cakes; you can make the marzipan yourself or buy it ready-made. The fruits make a very pretty addition to a cake or, if presented attractively in a small box, a pleasant gift. You can

1 ✼ Dust the eggcup well with cornflour (US cornstarch). Roll out a little white modelling paste and fit it into the eggcup. Work the paste until it is an even thickness. Shape it to fit, making a neat barrel shape.
2 ✼ Trim the top edge and carefully take the little barrel out of the eggcup. Re-dust the cup with cornflour and put the barrel back in to dry.
3 ✼ Paint brown.
4 ✼ Make tiny, twisted 'ropes' to go around the top and bottom of the barrel. Attach with a little water and leave to dry.
5 ✼ Paint the twists a darker brown than the barrel.

Floodwork

There are endless ways of using this type of cake decoration as well as many different designs. What you are actually doing is reproducing an existing design in royal icing. Cards and pictures can be used as models. I find this method particularly useful when decorating a cake for a man. His hobbies, sporting interests and work can all be portrayed in a bold and interesting way.

There are 3 methods of doing floodwork.

Materials

You will need a card or picture, preferably in colour, of the design you wish to reproduce (the work will be made easier if you have 2 copies of the design), uncreased waxed paper, sticky tape, a pencil, royal icing, a size 00 tube, lemon juice, and a 30 cm (12 in) board.

Method 1 — Traditional

1 ✻ Tape the design to the board with sticky tape. Do not allow the tape to touch any part of the design.

2 ✻ Cover the design with waxed paper, with the waxed side facing up, and tape it down.

3 ✻ Using a lead pencil, outline the design, which should be visible through the waxed paper, onto the waxed paper.

4 ✻ Using royal icing of piping consistency, outline the design on the waxed paper. Allow to dry.

5 ✳ Pipe a second row of icing on top of the first outline.

6 ✳ To fill in the area between the outlines, use royal icing mixed with lemon juice. The flatter and smoother the texture of the design, the more lemon juice you will need. You can use white royal icing and colour it once it has dried, or colour the icing before using it. If you only have a small area to cover, it is simpler to use white icing and paint it later. Black areas should always be made with white royal icing, then painted when dry with black food colouring straight from the bottle.

Using a paintbrush and palette knife, fill in and cover the outline. Make the icing either smooth or rough, depending on the design (eg, eyes are smooth and round, Father Christmas's beard is thick and fluffy). Always allow one colour to dry before applying the next, otherwise the stronger colour will bleed into the paler one.

7 ✳ When you have completed the filling in process — the flooding — remove the design and use it as a guide for painting in the fine details. This is where a second copy of the design can be useful.

When the floodwork is completely dry, and just before you are ready to place it on top of the cake, remove the waxed paper.

Note
Always use a pale colour to fill in an animal shape; hair also, whether it is dark or fair. The colour can be adjusted with food colouring painted on later. Use red powdered food colouring to get a Christmas red and always mix well. Remember that you are actually creating a 3-dimensional plaque. To get this effect, you will need to contour any human bodies that are in the design. Give the face a nose, eyebrows, a moustache etc, by applying royal icing once the face is dry.

Method 2 — Run-in Floodwork
1 ✳ Trace your design onto greaseproof paper.
2 ✳ Turn the paper over and trace the back. Turn the paper back over and trace the design carefully onto a dried plaque of modelling fondant.

3 ✳ Choose the colours you need. Mix some of each with royal icing and a little water, and keep covered.
4 ✳ Start to fill in the design on the plaque, beginning with the area furthest away from you. Let each area dry before proceeding to the next one, gradually working your way to the front of the design. Leave to dry.
5 ✳ Paint in the details using the original design as a guide. You can paint in grass and flowers if you wish, and use small moulded or piped flowers to enhance the picture.

Method 3 — Moulded Work

This is certainly the quickest way, but you will need good moulds. For a Father Christmas face:

1 ✳ Dust the inside of the mould with cornflour (US cornstarch). Roll out white modelling paste and press into the mould, being careful to follow its contours. Remove any excess paste.

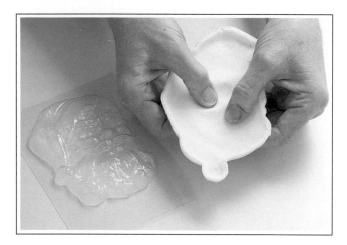

2 ✳ Take the face out, re-dust the mould with cornflour and replace the face. Allow to dry.

3 ✳ Using royal icing, pipe in the details of the beard and cap. Paint in the features of the face.

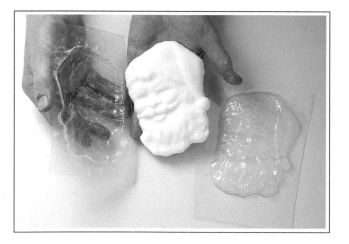

Ornaments

MOULDED BOOTEES

This method was thought of by one of my students, and can be used as a decoration for a christening cake. There are 3 pieces in the pattern — the sole, the toe and the heel.

Method

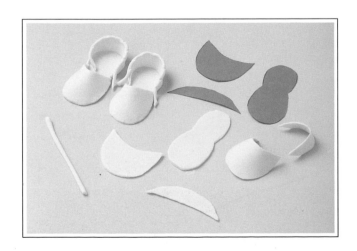

1 ✲ Cut out 2 soles in white or coloured modelling paste and dry flat. Do not make them bigger than the template (see p 137), although you can make them smaller.

2 ✲ Cut out 2 toes. Dampen the edges and fit around the front part of the sole, shaping the toe up and over as you go.

3 ✠ Cut out 2 heels. Dampen the edges and fit around the back part of the sole. Allow the shoes to dry.

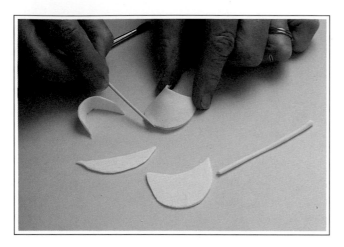

4 ✠ Make a flat strap, or roll out some paste to make a shoe strap. Attach to the heel so that it looks ready to be either buttoned or tied. Attach a pearl stamen for the button. Allow to dry.

5 ✠ If you have made the bootees in white paste, paint them with food colouring mixed with pure alcohol. This will give a softer colour. You can decorate the bootees with scattered forget-me-nots, groups of small dots, or a tiny bow at the centre of the toe arch.

BIBLE OR BOOK

A Bible or prayer book with some flowers make a very pretty decoration for the top of a wedding cake. The following directions are for one on the top of a cake; a smaller version would be suitable for the centre of a bottom tier.

If you are making a Communion cake, use the prayer book and add some rosary beads. If you want a plain Bible, the covering must be done very well. The one in the photograph was imprinted with guipure lace and embroidered with royal icing.

Method

1 ✠ Cut out a block of white modelling paste 7½ x 5 cm (3 x 2 in) and 9 mm (⅜ in) thick.
2 ✠ Trim 1¼ cm (½ in) off the longer side and make into a roll.
3 ✠ Re-attach the roll to the block so that it looks like the curved back of a book.

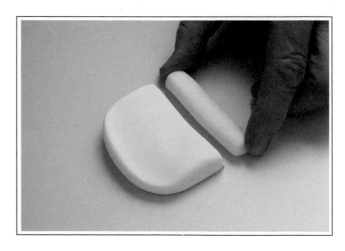

4 ✠ Roll out a rectangle of paste 11¼ x 7½ cm (4½ x 3 in) and no more than 3 mm (⅛ in) thick.

5 ✳ Gently press some guipure lace over one-half of the length so that its imprint is in the paste. Peel away.

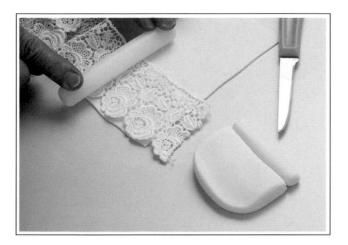

6 ✳ Lift up the paste (with the design facing outwards) and wrap it around the block of paste. Start at one edge, curling it around the roll at the back and finish at the other edge.

7 ✳ Mark the length of the book to define where the paste covers the roll so that you have a clearly defined spine on the book.

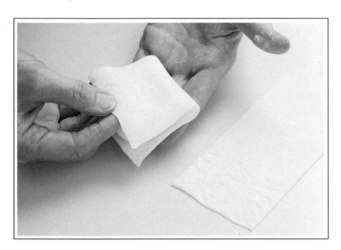

8 ✳ Make 3 horizontal marks across the roll to delegate a space for the title, author etc.

9 ✳ Using a sharp knife, mark the end of the book that would open so that it looks like paper pages.

10 ✳ Fill in the pattern of the lace with piped royal icing.

11 ✳ Attach a 7½ cm (3 in) length of ribbon that is ½ cm (¼ in) wide as a book mark.

BIBS

A bib is quick and easy to make. It can be the sole decoration on a 20 cm (8 in) christening cake, and is appropriate for a boy or a girl. Make it in coloured modelling paste if you wish, or in white paste that you spray with colour later.

Method 1

1 ✳ Use the template (see p 137) to cut out the bib in cardboard.

2 ✳ Place the cardboard pattern on rolled-out paste and cut out. Be certain not to drag or tear the paste — if you do, you will alter the shape.

3 ✳ Decorate the edges. You can do this by using either a leatherwork tool for making designs or the top of a teaspoon handle that has an interesting pattern. Alternatively, you can leave the shape plain and decorate it with royal icing later. Tuck a small wad of waxed paper under 2 or 3 of the scalloped shapes around the edge. This will help to flute them upwards and create a flowing effect.

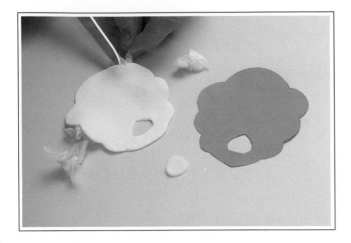

4 ✢ When completely dry, decorate the whole bib. You can write 'Baby' or the child's name, and work a design around the first letter.

Method 2

1 ✢ Make 2 bibs using the smaller template (see p 137). Cut the bottom one from paste approximately ½ cm (¼ in) thick. Roll out the top one as finely as possible.

2 ✢ Flute and decorate the edges of the top bib.

3 ✢ Place the top bib over the thicker bib. Attach them around the neck area.

4 ✢ Decorate the rest of the top bib. Place sprays of tiny flowers so that they emerge from under the area that lifts away from the bottom bib. Finish around the neck with piping. Attach a very small bow.

KNITTED BOOTEES

The idea for these came from a knitting book. All the work is done in royal icing of petal consistency. Do follow the pattern carefully. You can use white or coloured modelling paste.

Method

1 ✢ Cut 2 template shapes (see p 137) from modelling paste 3¾ cm (1½ in) long and 2½ cm (1 in) thick.

2 ✢ Poke 2 holes in the bottom of each bootee to enable the paste to dry without splitting.

3 ✢ Fill a No 8 star tube with royal icing the same colour as the paste. Pipe a row of stars around the ankle using a pull–push movement.

4 ✢ Pipe 3 flat lines about 1 cm (½ in) long from the ankle out towards the toe area.

5 ✢ With a No 8 star tube, pipe vertical lines right around the heel. Pipe from one side indent to the other, keeping the lines so close together that no paste shows through.

6 ✢ By now, the first row of stars around the ankle will be dry. Pipe a second row of stars on top of the first row. Leave to dry. Pipe a third and then a fourth row. Make sure each row is dry before working on the next one.

7 ✢ Hold the bootee up. Beginning in the middle of the bootee, where the 3 flat lines finish, use a No 12 star tube to pipe a line over the toe to the sole. Continue making these lines until the front half of the bootee is completely covered and no paste shows through.

8 ✢ Use a contrasting colour to pipe around the area where the flat lines and the toe lines meet. Work in a half circle, using a push–pull action.

9 ✷ Pipe a fifth row of stars around the ankle in the contrasting colour.

10 ✷ Decorate the bootee with a tiny bow.

11 ✷ Make the other bootee to match.

CHRISTMAS CRACKER

Method

1 ✷ Make a cylinder of modelling paste (using whatever colour you wish) that is 2½ cm (1 in) long and 9 mm (⅜ in) thick. Make a hole in each end so that it can dry thoroughly.

2 ✷ Roll out an oblong piece of paste that is 3 times the length of the cylinder and wide enough to encircle it with an overlapping piece.

3 ✷ Mark the ends of the oblong with a pattern, which will be painted in later. Turn paste over.

4 ✷ Place the cylinder of paste in the middle of the oblong piece. Gently roll the oblong piece over the cylinder so that it is now enclosed in a long outer cylinder.

5 ✷ Squeeze the outer cylinder very gently at either end of the enclosed cylinder to make a typical Christmas cracker shape.

6 ✷ Put your forefingers down into the narrowed shapes at either end. Push the two ends together very, very gently.

7 ✷ Paint in the pattern on the ends. Attach stars, cut-out flowers or any other suitable decoration to the body of the cracker.

FIREPLACE

This is something different for a Christmas cake. I made up my first one as I went along, but this one I copied from a card. You could make up your own design quite easily if you wanted to.

Method

1 ✷ Cut an oblong piece of paste 1 cm (½ in) thick and of an appropriate size. You can use white modelling paste and paint it later, or a coloured paste — terracotta for bricks, soft yellow for slate.

2 ✷ Cut out a half circle arch low down in the centre of the block of paste but be careful not to cut through to the back of the paste. Either mark the paste with a scalpel to show the bricks or stones, or leave it plain. Dry flat.

3 ✶ You can, if you wish, make a second arch of bricks and place this over the first.

4 ✶ Make the mantelpiece from a sausage of paste the same thickness. Flatten. Place it along the top of the fireplace to form the mantelpiece.

How much decoration or variation you add now is entirely up to you. You can paint in a fire grate, coal and flames, or mould a vase of flowers for the mantelpiece, or a coal bucket or copper hood for the fireplace. Don't forget the holly and berries to give a festive touch.

WISHING WELL

This pretty ornament can be used on a birthday cake. It is only small, so you will need to add some flowers as an accompaniment. You will need 2 tools to cut out a circle approximately 2½ cm (1 in) in diameter and another circle approximately 1 cm (⅜ in) in diameter. I use a very small jam jar for the first circle and an empty glass phial that used to contain glitter dust for the second. You will also need some toothpicks (wooden picks) and a matchbox bottom.

Well

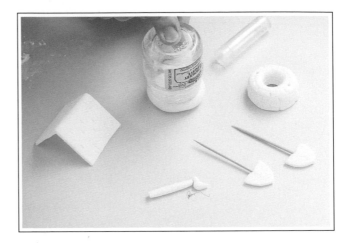

1 ✶ Roll out a ball of modelling paste 3 cm (1¼ in) in diameter and 1¼ cm (½ in) thick.

2 ✶ Use cornflour (US cornstarch) to dust the rim of the jam jar and use it as a mould to create the well. Make certain the cut is clean.

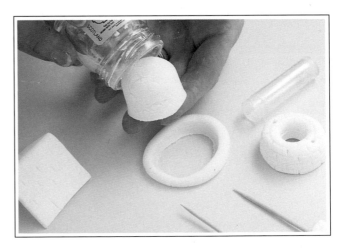

3 ✶ Use the smaller cutting tool to cut a hole in the centre of this circle of paste. Remove the surplus paste.

4 ✶ Mark in brickwork around the circle of paste with a scalpel.

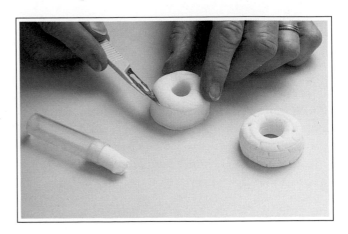

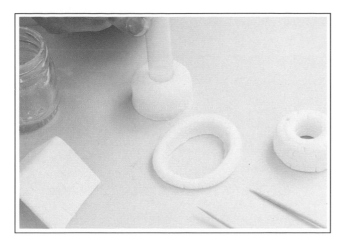

5 ✶ Insert 1 toothpick in the top rim of the paste and another one directly opposite it. These will hold the roof of the well in position. Keep turning the toothpicks to prevent them from sticking to the paste as it dries. You will need to be able to remove them later. Leave the well to dry.

6 ✶ Paint the well and allow to dry.

Roof

1 ✶ Roll out a piece of modelling paste 5 x 7½ cm (2 x 3 in) and 3 mm (⅛ in) thick.

2 ✶ Mark in the roof slates with a scalpel. Start at the edge of the long sides and work inwards, leaving a blank space in the centre for the capping.

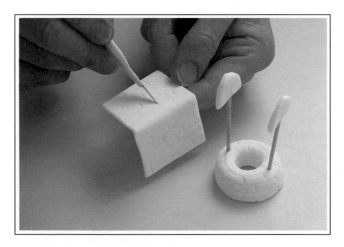

3 ✶ Fit the roof into the matchbox bottom, with the slats facing downwards. Place one side along the bottom of the box and gently bend the paste so that it stands upright against the side. Support it with a cottonwool ball. Allow to dry.

4 ✶ Paint the roof and allow to dry.

Side Structure

1 ✶ Cut 2 shapes from a piece of modelling paste ½ cm (¼ in) thick. Insert a toothpick in each one. Leave enough of the toothpicks protruding so that when they are fitted into the holes in the well, the roof will sit at the right height.

2 ✶ Place the side structures on a flat surface and leave to dry.

3 ✶ Paint the side structures and leave to dry.

Assembly

1 ✶ Position the toothpicks of the side structures in the holes in the well. Make sure they are level. Secure with royal icing.

2 ✶ Attach the roof using royal icing. Leave to dry.

3 ✶ Roll a tiny piece of white paste about 3 mm (⅛ in) thick. It must be long enough to run from one toothpick to the other with a small piece extending at either end. Attach about halfway down the toothpicks with royal icing. This forms the 'piece of wood' to which a bucket and rope would be attached. Leave to dry.

4 ✠ Pipe a rope around the 'piece of wood', leaving an end which can be attached to a bucket.

5 ✠ Decorate the well with vines and flowers, either moulded or piped.

BELLS

A bell for a wedding cake is long and slender; a Christmas bell is wider and more solid-looking, and has a shoulder. Moulds are available in either plastic, glass or brass. You can mould the bell by fitting paste around the outside of the mould and making a neat join. Alternatively, you can shape the paste on the inside of the bell, in which case the bell will have no join. However, you will find it more difficult to make a paste that is thin enough while still being able to hold its shape. The first method is the one I describe below.

Method

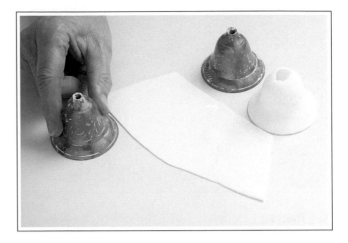

1 ✠ Dust the outside of the mould with cornflour (US cornstarch).

2 ✠ Roll out the paste thinly and cut into a rough bell shape.

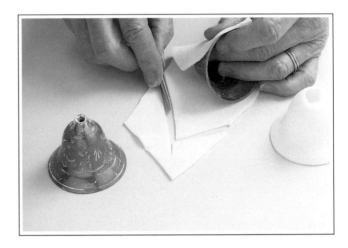

3 ✠ Fold around the mould until the 2 sides meet. Remove it from the mould and trim away any excess paste.

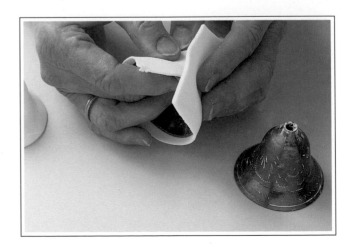

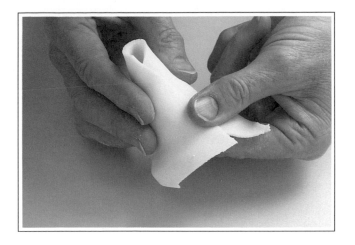

4 ✸ Re-dust the mould with cornflour and replace the paste bell. Dampen the paste at the edge of the join and smooth to make the join as invisible as possible.

6 ✸ Take the paste bell off the mould again and re-dust the mould to make sure they do not stick together. Replace the paste and make your final shaping.

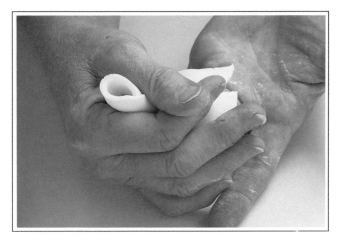

5 ✸ Ease the paste slightly at both the top and bottom ends and cut away the excess.

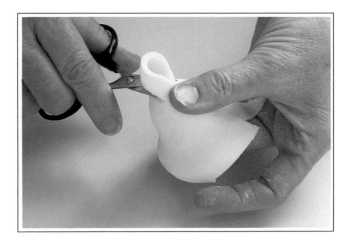

7 ✸ While the paste is still damp, you can use tiny flower cutters to cut out shapes on the bell. Make sure the cuts are clean.

8 ✸ Remove the paste bell from the mould once it is dry and make sure that there is no cornflour attached to the inside of the bell.

9 ✸ Decorate the inside with cornelli or with a pattern of tiny dots.

10 ✸ To make an edging around the bottom of the bell, mark the bottom into 16 equal sections with a dot of royal icing. Pipe loops of royal icing between these dots. Allow to dry then pipe another layer of icing on top of these loops. Do this twice more so that the scallops stand away from the edge of the bell. Allow to dry.

11 ✵ With a fine tube, pipe threadwork from the bell out to the scallops, giving you an extension finish on the bottom edge of your bell. Finish the bottom scallop with a tiny snail's trail. Finish the top edge with tiny loops. Place a forget-me-not with a coloured stamen head in the centre of the bell above the top edging of the extension.

12 ✵ Close up the top of the bell with royal icing.

13 ✵ If the bell is less than 7½ cm (3 in) in size, use 2 bells. Fill them with small sprays of filler flowers, small pieces of soft tulle and ribbon. Place them together on their sides with small sprays of filler flowers between them and with loops of stiff ribbon behind them.

SLIPPERS

This method can be used to make bootees, ballet shoes, football boots etc. Don't make the slippers too big, because they become hard to mould and to match.

Method

1 ✵ Roll a sausage of modelling paste 10 cm (4 in) long and 4 cm (1½ in) in diameter.

2 ✵ Flatten along the top.

3 ✵ Cut the block into 2 pieces, matching in length and height. Round the toe area.

4 ✵ Take a round-ended piece of dowel, 2 cm (¾ in) in diameter, and push it into the block at a point about halfway down the block. Push it into the toe area.

5 ✵ Mould the toe area over the piece of dowel and pull up the tongue.

6 ✵ Turn the dowel towards the heel and work out the foot and heel area.

7 ✵ Smooth out the inside of the slipper.

8 ✵ Paint with food colouring straight from the bottle. Trim with a royal icing shell, frilled to represent fur.

Chocolate

This is a fun area of cake decorating. You can use pure chocolate or compound chocolate — it is very important to understand the difference. Pure chocolate must be at exactly the right temperature while you are working with it, otherwise it sticks to the mould and turns white as it dries. This is because the cocoa butter in the mixture has separated. Compound chocolate will not do this. The cocoa butter has been extracted and replaced by oil, which allows it to come out of the mould easily. Compound chocolate is not as smooth as the real thing, but I have found that combining 500 g (1 lb) of compound chocolate with 375 g (12 oz) of pure chocolate gives a mixture that works very well and has a lovely taste. You can make moulded chocolates, flowers, leaves and, of course, Easter eggs.

The photographs show leaves that are made by painting melted chocolate onto a real leaf. When the chocolate is dry, it peels off easily. There are also photographs of chocolates made in moulds in 2 colours. The chocolates with the white bloom were made from melted chocolate that was the wrong temperature. The other photograph shows filling such as peanuts, sultanas (golden raisins) and cream centres that have been dipped in melted chocolate.

Easter Eggs

You can buy plastic moulds with which to make the eggs. Fill one-half of the mould with melted chocolate.

Clip on the other half of the mould, matching the edges carefully so that the chocolate will not spurt out.

Turn the closed mould round and round so that the chocolate coats the whole of the inside of the mould as evenly as possible.

Place it in the refrigerator and leave until it is really cold. When you open the mould, the chocolate egg should lift out easily.

Chocolate for Piping

Add 1–2 drops of glycerine to 60 g (2 oz) melted compound chocolate. This thickens the chocolate to make it suitable for lace, scrolls, latticework and writing. Use a cellophane cornet bag with the point cut out to make an opening of the required size.

You will need to work more quickly than you would when using royal icing, as chocolate hardens faster. If the chocolate becomes too hard to pipe, place it in a microwave oven for 2 seconds to bring it back to a piping consistency.

Chocolate for Moulding

Add 2 teaspoons of warmed liquid glucose or 2 teaspoons of corn syrup to 60 g (2 oz) melted compound chocolate. Mix thoroughly. Wrap in plastic wrap (cling film) and leave in the refrigerator for about 1 hour before using.

Cakes for Special Occasions

PINK OVAL BIRTHDAY CAKE

This small oval cake can be made very quickly. It is one of the easiest ways of decorating a small cake, and some very pretty effects can be created. The plaque is cocoa-painted.

Plaque

1 ✲ Cut out the shape of the plaque in modelling paste and leave to dry thoroughly. Keep turning it over for a few days until both sides are completely dry.

2 ✲ Trace your chosen design onto greaseproof paper. Turn it over and pencil the design in on the back. Place the back side of the paper onto the dry plaque and trace the design as lightly and clearly as possible.

3 ✲ Melt 2 teaspoons of cocoa butter (obtainable from a chemist (drug store)) in a small container over hot water and add a little cocoa powder. Do not mix all the powder in. Keep it pale to begin with, for the light parts of the design. You can mix in more cocoa powder later for the darker areas. Paint in the design using the lighter and darker butter as needed.

4 ✲ Allow the painted plaque to dry. Be sure not to touch any of the painted parts with your fingers.

BOY'S CHRISTENING CAKE

Baby-blue fondant covers this cake, which has teddy bears as its theme. The little ones on the top are made from modelling paste with piped royal icing for the fur. You could also make the bears from marzipan if you wished. The bear on the side of the cake and the lettering is floodwork. The nylon ribbon around the side is dyed with brown food colouring mixed with pure alcohol to match the colours of the bears. The tiny flower sprays are made up of primulas (see p 41) and bluebells.

Teddy Bears

1 ✿ Mould a pear-shaped piece of modelling paste to make the body of the bear. Insert a round toothpick (wooden pick) into the neck, with enough protruding so that the head can be attached.

2 ✿ Make the arms and legs from little sausages of paste. Nip them in to form the wrists and ankles, and flatten the ends for the paws and feet.

3 ✿ Attach to the body with a little water.

4 ✿ Make the head from a much smaller pear-shaped piece of paste. Shape the nose and make little indentations for the eyes. Mould 2 ears. Make a slit on either side of the head and fit the ears into them.

5 ✿ Make 2 holes in the underside of the body so that the paste can dry evenly. Leave until the body is completely dry.

6 ✿ Use royal icing to pipe short, downward strokes all over the bear, to create the fur.

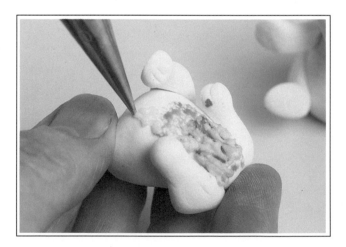

7 ✿ Fill in the eye indentations with a little royal icing. Leave to dry.

8 ✿ Paint the bear a light caramel-brown with food colouring mixed with water. Paint in the details of the eyes, nose and mouth with food colouring straight from the bottle.

Bluebells

1 ✠ Hollow out a 5 mm (¼ in) cone made from pale blue modelling paste.

2 ✠ Make 5 short cuts into the rim of the cone to create 5 petals of equal size.

3 ✠ Mitre each petal to a point.

4 ✠ Place the round end of the ball tool down into the cone to give the bell shape.

5 ✠ Wire with a knotted end on the wire.

DAPHNE CAKE

This pretty cake is suitable for a birthday, anniversary or engagement cake. Instructions for making the daphnes are found on p 66. The side design can be of your own choosing, but remember to cut a template for a cake of this shape so that the design is in perspective. The embroidery should flow with the design.

GIRL'S CHRISTENING CAKE

The frill is made by using an 8-petal daisy cutter. Make the modelling paste as fine as possible. Roll the petals with a toothpick (wooden pick) and leave to dry on a curved surface. There are 6 template pieces for the cradle.

Cradle

1 ✠ Cut out template pieces 1, 2 and 3 from white modelling paste. Cut out two of piece 4.

2 ✠ Dry pieces 1, 2 and 4 flat.

3 ✠ While piece 3 is still damp, turn up both sides by about 1 cm (½ in). Support as it dries. This forms the bed part of the cradle.

4 ✠ Attach the ends of piece 3 to the bottom half of piece 1 with a thread of royal icing. Allow to dry.

5 ✠ Attach piece 2 to the other end of piece 3 in the same way. Make sure the cradle is level and will rock. Allow to dry.

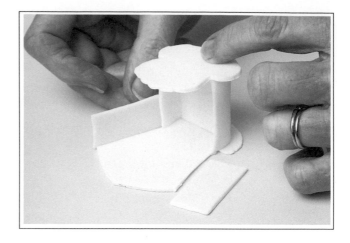

6 ✠ Attach both side pieces — piece 4 — and allow to dry.

7 ✠ Lie the cradle on its back. Cut out piece 5. While it is still damp, mould it around the top of the cradle and join to the side pieces. Allow to dry.

8 ✠ Mix brown food colouring with pure alcohol and paint the cradle to create the effect of wood.

9 ✠ Mould a baby pillow from a ball of fondant. Round both ends and half-flatten.

10 ✛ To make a baby cover, roll a thin piece of fondant 5 cm (2 in) square. Mark with small squares, using the back of a knife. While still wet, place in cradle. Leave to dry, then paint the squares in a range of pale colours.

11 ✛ Decorate the cradle with a garland of tiny flowers of mixed colours.

GIRL'S BIRTHDAY CAKE

I've developed something a bit different for this cake. I make the colour for the fondant covering by mixing caramel with a little green and chestnut-brown food colouring. The beads, bangles and earrings are made from white modelling paste and painted when the paste is dry. Bouvardia and primulas are the flowers around the base of the cake.

Bangles

1 ✛ Roll out a ball of modelling paste 2½ cm (1 in) in diameter. Use the rim of a small jam jar to cut a neat circle.

2 ✛ Use a smaller jar (eg, a pill phial) to cut out the centre of the circle. Gently lift it out and discard.

3 ✛ Mould the circle of paste with your fingers to make a bangle. Paint when dry.

TRAIN

Jam rolls and rollettes, liquorice, chocolate biscuits (cookies), buttercream and plenty of colourful lollies (sweets, candy) are used to make the train. Just follow the photograph.

Buttercream Recipe

75–125 g (3–4 oz) butter, softened
1¼–1½ cups (200–250 g, 7–8 oz) icing (confectioner's, powdered) sugar
2 teaspoons lemon juice
liquid food colouring
¼ cup (25 g, 1 oz) cocoa powder (optional)
sweet sherry to taste (optional)

Method

Beat the butter in an electric mixer on medium speed. Add 2 teaspoons of icing sugar at a time until the mixture (batter) is light and fluffy. Mix in lemon juice. Colour with liquid food colouring. If you do not use the mixture at once, keep it in the refrigerator. Take it out 12 hours before you wish to use it to allow it to come to room temperature.

To make Vienna cream, mix 3 tablespoons of cocoa powder into a smooth paste with some sweet sherry. Add to the basic buttercream mixture and stir well.

DOLLY VARDEN CAKE FOR A LITTLE GIRL

Quick Version

Make a basic butter cake in a Dolly Varden tin (pan). Allow to cool. You now need a 9 cm (3½ in) doll with legs, and with or without hair. Push the doll down into the centre of the cake so that the

cake reaches its waist and becomes the skirt. Decorating is now up to you.

You can use buttercream and different-sized star tubes to pipe the skirt design and the top of the dress. You can adorn the head with a little piped icing; place a flower in the doll's hand and surround the base with colourful lollies (sweets, candy) — which may prove to be the most important part of the cake. This is all very quick and simple to do. A bow of ribbon completes the effect.

Detailed Version

If you wish to take more time and trouble, cover a fruit cake with fondant and decorate it as a nursery rhyme figure, an old-fashioned lady, a Dutch girl — the variety is endless. Be prepared though — it will involve hours of work, and the cake will be eaten just as quickly as the cake prepared using the quick version!

FATHER'S DAY CAKE

This is a rectangular cake with a card of moulded tools as the theme. The colour of the fondant covering is a mixture of sky-blue with a touch of mauve. The sides are simply a shell border and 2 strands of narrow burgundy-coloured ribbon. Light embroidery that depicts sports can enhance the Father's Day theme.

WOODEN WALL CARD

1 ✠ Make a card in modelling paste approximately 12½ x 7½ cm (5 x 3 in) and 3 mm (⅛ in) thick.

2 ✠ Mark in wood grain with a ruler.

3 ✠ Make nail holes while the paste is wet.

4 ✠ Leave to dry flat, turning over every 24 hours.

5 ✠ When dry, paint with brown food colouring to give the appearance of a wooden wall.

Tools

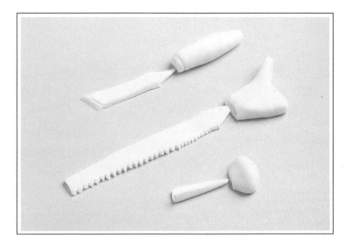

These can be of your own choosing; maybe they can represent a particular trade.

1 ✠ Mould each tool, making sure that you keep them in proportion.

2 ✠ When dry, paint the handles in a darker brown than you have used for the card.

3 ✠ Paint all iron parts in silver paint. This is not easy to obtain, but you can buy gold and silver felt pens which are non-toxic. Allow to dry.

4 ✠ Attach tools to the card with royal icing. Allow to dry.

POINSETTIA CHRISTMAS CAKE

This 20 cm (8 in) square cake covered in white fondant has a poinsettia as its main decoration. A scroll, a Christmas rose, holly leaves and cones, shells and a leaf, all made from modelling paste, add to the effect. The side design is piped from a bag of royal icing that has a streak of red and green down the inside, so that the icing is variegated in the Christmas colours. Thin, red ribbon adds the final touch.

Poinsettia

1 ✠ Make twenty 2½ cm (1 in) long beans of red modelling paste. Shape them to a longish point at both ends.
2 ✠ Flatten them and widen in the middle.

3 ✠ Draw in veins with the back of a knife. They are leaves, not petals.
4 ✠ Make 10 tiny, green, paste gumnuts (see p 89). Leave to dry.
5 ✠ Pat a dob of royal icing in the centre of a square of waxed paper.
6 ✠ Make the shape of the poinsettia, using 2 rows of red leaves, by placing the lower points in the royal icing.
7 ✠ Fill the centre of each poinsettia with gumnuts, which are also filled with royal icing. Leave to dry.
8 ✠ Colour the gumnuts a darker green. Paint the icing inside them in yellow, with a speck of red.

WOMAN'S TWENTY-FIRST BIRTHDAY CAKE

The fondant covering is a soft lemon-yellow. For the spray I have chosen pretty field flowers with some wheat. Two different lace patterns are used in the design that includes the small keys to represent the coming of age.

Buttercups

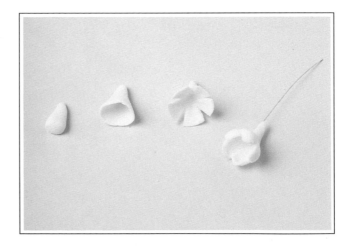

1 ✠ Hollow out a 2 cm (¾ in) long cone of modelling paste quite widely.
2 ✠ Make 5 long cuts in the rim to form the petals.
3 ✠ Mitre the edges of the petals to make them round.
4 ✠ Using a large ball tool, roll each petal sideways and lengthways, cupping them gently.

5 ✤ Ease the petals inwards so that they overlap and make a cupped flower.

6 ✤ Place a tiny dot of royal icing in the centre. Fill with stamen threads.

7 ✤ Paint the petals with bright yellow food colouring straight from the bottle. Tip each stamen thread with brown food colouring.

Poppies

1 ✤ Make 5 Dainty Bess petals (see p 35) about 2½ cm (1 in) long. Flute the top edge of the petal gently and leave to dry.

2 ✤ Paint the bottom quarter of the petal yellow and leave to dry.

3 ✤ Paint the rest of the petal pillar-box red. Allow to dry.

4 ✤ Touch the dried, yellow part of the petal with a little green colour. Wipe this off and touch over with the red colour, so that only a point of yellow remains.

5 ✤ Place the 5 petals in the poppy shape and hold in place with a little royal icing. Leave space for a moulded centre to be inserted.

6 ✤ Make a very small cone of modelling paste. Flatten the top and mark with a cross.

7 ✤ Insert the moulded centre in the middle of the petals and surround with black stamens. Use royal icing to keep in place.

8 ✤ Pipe over the cross with royal icing and, while it is wet, dust with yellow chalk.

FORTIETH WEDDING ANNIVERSARY CAKE

Ruby-red and white are the colours to use for this anniversary cake. I have chosen roses, white fillers, and used floodwork for the number '40'. Frills and tiny loops make up the side design.

Number Figures

1 ✤ Trace a '4' and '0' onto greaseproof paper. Space them apart.
2 ✤ Cover with waxed paper and outline with royal icing, using a size 00 tube. Leave to dry.
3 ✤ Fill in with royal icing mixed with a little water. Brush lightly to make the filling smooth and even. Allow to dry.

4 ✤ Paint with pillar-box red food colouring straight from the bottle.
5 ✤ When dry, edge the numbers with royal icing dots. Make 2 dots close together, leave a space, then pipe 2 more dots. Continue this around the numbers. When dry, pipe another dot between each set of 2 dots.
6 ✤ Lift the numbers when completely dry and place on the cake.

ONE-TIER WEDDING CAKE

This oval cake is covered in a soft, cream fondant. The plaque is run-in floodwork and the flowers around the edge of the plaque are open roses and pink apple blossoms.

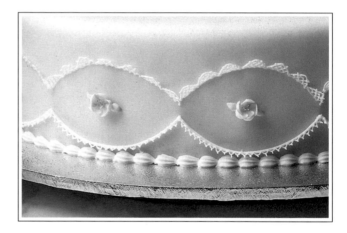

The open roses are made from Dainty Bess petals (see p 35). Paint the back with pale pink food colouring mixed with pure alcohol.

The decoration is completed by 4 rows of scallops around the side of the cake. Lacework and tiny apple blossoms are placed in the centre of this.

Apple Blossom

1 ✳ Make 5 of the smallest Dainty Bess petals that you can (see p 35).

2 ✳ Use the round end of a hair-roller pin to cup each one. Allow to dry.

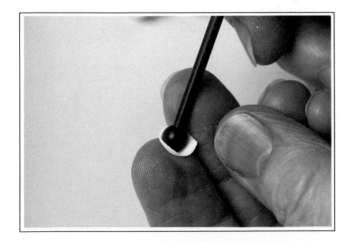

3 ✳ Place a very small dot of royal icing in the centre of a cup of waxed paper. Arrange the petals so that they overlap and the last one tucks behind the first one.

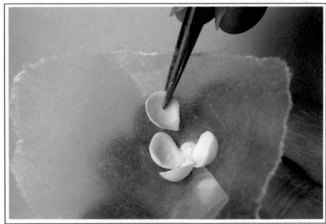

4 ✳ Insert 4–5 short stamen threads in the centre of the flower. Allow to dry.

5 ✳ Paint the back of the petals with pink food colouring mixed with pure alcohol. Tip the end of the stamen threads with burgundy food colouring.

TWO-TIER OCTAGONAL CAKE

This cake features the sweetheart rose (see p 57) and eriostemon as fillers. Dainty embroidery and extension work combined with lace insets (see p 135 for the design) complete the sides. The ring pillars are unusual and give an uncluttered look to the tiers.

Eriostemon Flower

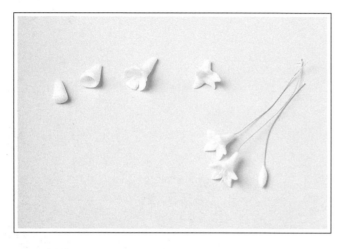

1 ✻ Make a ½ cm (¼ in) long cone of modelling paste. Hollow out finely.
2 ✻ Make 5 long cuts in the rim of the cone to create 5 petals.
3 ✻ Mitre each petal into a gentle point and flatten.

4 ✻ Wire and cup the petals gently.
5 ✻ Place 3 short stamen threads in the centre of the little, cupped flower. Leave to dry.

6 ✻ Paint only the back of the flower with pink food colouring mixed with pure alcohol.
7 ✻ Paint the stamen threads a soft yellow and leave to dry thoroughly.
8 ✻ Tip the very top of the thread with a speck of brown.

Eriostemon Buds

1 ✻ Make a longish bud from modelling paste and wire. Allow to dry.
2 ✻ Paint with pink food colouring mixed with pure alcohol. Leave to dry.
3 ✻ Paint on a very pale green calyx.

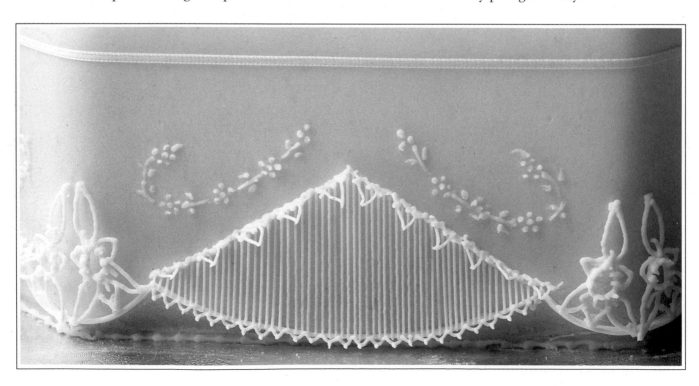

THREE-TIER WEDDING CAKE

Each piece of lace covering the ribbon at the base of this hexagonal-shaped cake is made separately. The method for making lace is described on p 25. When dry, lift carefully and place over the ribbon. Attach it carefully with royal icing. The small flowers in the spray are rosebuds (see p 54), primulas (p 41), hyacinths (p 46) and bouvardia. A dovecote, surrounded by sprays of the same small flowers, decorates the top of the cake.

Dovecote

1 ❈ Use the template to cut the front, the back and the 2 side pieces of the dovecote from white modelling paste (see p 136). Dry flat.

2 ❈ While the front is still damp, cut out a small circle to make the entrance to the dovecote.

3 ❈ Attach the 2 sides to the front with a little royal icing. Allow to dry.

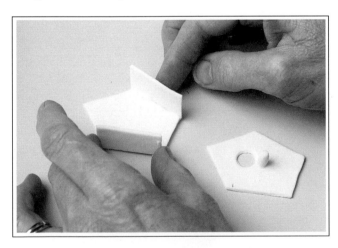

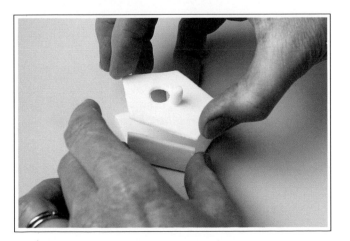

4 ❈ Attach the back to the 2 sides with a little royal icing. Make sure everything is level and that the dovecote will stand up safely. Allow to dry.

5 ❈ Cut a strip of modelling paste ½ cm (¼ in) wider than the roof area with a ½ cm (¼ in) overlap at either end.

6 ❈ Attach at once with royal icing to the top of the 4 walls of the dovecote to make a neat roof. Allow to dry.

7 ❈ Make a base of modelling paste that is 1¼ cm (½ in) larger than the dovecote base all around. Dry flat.

8 ❈ Attach the dovecote to this base with a little royal icing.

9 ❈ Make a very small perch in modelling paste. When dry, attach to the dovecote just under the hole in the front.

10 ❈ Make 2 small birds. Make sure they are in proportion to the dovecote and not too heavy. Attach one bird to the perch and one to the base.

11 ❈ Roll out a piece of modelling paste 2½ x 1¼ cm (1 x ½ in). This is a stand for the dovecote. Allow to dry. Attach the whole dovecote to it using royal icing.

12 ❈ Decorate the dovecote with piped royal icing to show the tiles on the roof and the patterning on the walls.

BIRTHDAY CAKE

The avocado colour of the fondant goes well with the golden-yellow of the hibbertia, which is a very easy flower to make.

Hibbertia Flower

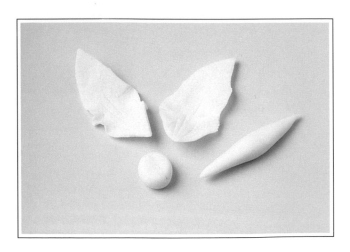

1 ✠ Mix yellow and a spot of peach food colouring into white modelling paste to give the hibbertia colour.

2 ✠ Make a bean of paste 2 cm (¾ in) long, which is pointed at each end. Flatten and thin out, widening the petal in the middle.

3 ✠ Press a small pad of crepe paper into the petal to give it texture.

4 ✠ Make 4–5 marks down the length of the petal with a knife.

5 ✠ Flute both sides of the bottom half of the petal with your fingers.

6 ✠ Turn over and roll the top half of both sides of the central vein with a ball tool. Make 5 petals for each flower.

Hibbertia Centre

1 ✠ Take a ball of yellow fondant and half-flatten it. This should now have a rolled appearance when viewed from the side view.

2 ✠ Insert half-headed stamens about 1 cm (⅜ in)

long, making sure you keep the rolled shape of the base. Use lots of stamens to fill the centre. It should be a good 1¼ cm (½ in) in diameter.

Assembly

1 ✶ Place a dot of royal icing on a square of waxed paper and place the first 3 petals at 1, 5 and 8 o'clock respectively. Place the fourth petal overlapping between the first and second petals. Place the last petal overlapping between the opposite 2 petals.

2 ✶ Insert the centre, making sure all the royal icing holding the petals in place is covered. The centre of the flower must be neat and clean.

3 ✶ Dry in patty tins (pans) for support.

AUSTRALIAN CHRISTMAS CAKE

The fondant covering of this cake is buff-coloured to highlight the colours of the wildflowers (see the section entitled 'Wildflowers'). The koala is done in floodwork. The holly leaves for the side decoration are done by drawing 2 holly leaves, placing waxed paper over the drawings and piping the design. Use a size 1 tube for strength, and keep the top level. Join the 2 leaves together at the top with berries to give support. Carefully lift the leaves and berries, and attach to the cake with a little royal icing.

OBLONG CAKE WITH FLANNEL FLOWERS

This cake features a Christmas card made from modelling paste and decorated with food colouring. It complements the spray of finely made flannel flowers that adorns the ribbon made from modelling paste.

To Make the Ribbon

1 ✠ Colour the paste with green food colouring and add a drop of yellow until it becomes a mossy green; then add a touch of blue.

This will give the colour of the flannel flower leaves.

2 ✠ Roll out the paste quickly to a thickness of 4 mm (⅛ in). Using a straight edge and a very sharp knife (be careful to avoid drag) cut a length to reach from the base of one side of the cake, across the length of the cake and down to the base on the

other side. Cut the second piece long enough to reach from base to base across the width of the cake. Secure with royal icing. Finish the edges with sets of three dots piped with a size 00 tube.

To Make the Card

1 ✠ You will need a pattern press of the design you have chosen.

2 ✠ Roll out the modelling paste finely. It should be long enough to take the design and leave a margin around to form a folded card shape.

3 ✠ Press in the pattern on the side that will be the front of the card; fold over and leave to dry.

4 ✠ When dry paint in all the colour and details of the Christmas scene.

5 ✠ Finish the edge with some fine pipe work.

To Make Flannel Flowers

1 ✠ Wire a ball of modelling paste, about 1½ cm (⅔ in) in size. Flatten the top and leave to dry.

2 ✤ Mix together some dry powdered gelatin and finely dusted moss-green chalk.

3 ✤ Paint the top half of the dried centre with green food colouring and while still damp dip it into the dry mixture. Allow to dry.

4 ✤ The petal shape is about 2 cm (¾ in) long, pointed at both ends, and widening in the centre area.

5 ✤ Only make two petals at a time and attach around the centre, moulding the base point well around the centre ball.

6 ✤ The real flower usually has 10 petals. It is difficult to place all 10 side by side, but they can overlap keeping the shape of the flower as true as possible.

7 ✤ The leaves are made from the same colour as the ribbon. Some are wired. There is a cutter available that is fairly close to the real shape of the leaf.

The base of the cake is finished with a bold shell made from a size 12 star tube.

OVAL CHRISTMAS BELL CAKE

This cake features brush-embroidered Christmas bells combined with moulded Christmas bells. The brush-embroidered Christmas bells sweep from under the moulded flowers down the face of the cake to the cake board. There is a smaller spray of flannel flowers on the opposite shoulder. To make the moulded flowers see pp 84, 91.

1 ✤ Trace the Christmas bell spray onto greaseproof paper, place under a piece of perspex and outline in royal icing with a size 1 tube.

2 ✤ When thoroughly dry and while the cake fondant is still soft, press it into place to leave an impression.

3 ✤ Using royal icing at a piping consistency, outline the shape of the bell and with a dampened brush gently work the thickness of the royal icing down to the pointed edge of the bell. Be sure to use

long even strokes and maintain the roundness at the base end of the bell.

4 ✷ When thoroughly dry the icing can then be coloured with food colouring mixed with a spirit (vodka, pure alcohol etc). Lastly pipe in details such as veins, stems etc.

5 ✷ A frill, about 3 cm (1¼ in) wide, made from modelling paste finishes the base edge. Leave a space to finish off the brush embroidery with a small moulded bell spray. The top edge of the frill is finished by pressing in a diamond-patterned plastic cutter into the cake and dotting the indentations in a pale green.

6 ✷ Cut out a small greeting card from modelling paste approximately 7 cm long and 3 cm wide (2¾ x 1¼ in). Cut each end at a slant and allow to dry. Either pipe or write (with a non-toxic pen) a greeting and place it in among the bells at an angle.

SQUARE WREATH CAKE

This cake consists of a Christmas wreath made up of miniature moulded Australian wildflowers, a tiny card with a greeting and 3 colour ribbons.

The flowers used in the wreath are 1 waratah, 4 flannel flowers, 2 sprays of Christmas bells with a bud, and 2 flowers 1 cm (½ in) long. To fill in around these main flowers are sprays of kurrajong, boronia and Christmas bush, with small holly leaves providing the base. For directions on making the wildflowers, see pp 81–93.

To Make the Wreath

1 ✷ Draw a circle with a diameter of 11 cm (4½ in), then draw another circle inside this with a diameter

of 7 cm (3 in). Cut out the centre leaving the 2 cm (¾ in) wide margin. This forms the base of the wreath.

2 ✳ Colour the modelling paste a dark green. Roll it out to a thickness of 7 mm (½ in). Place the circle pattern onto this and cut out with a sharp knife. Avoid dragging the paste because this distorts the shape. Allow to dry.

3 ✳ Cover the shape with holly leaves allowing some to face inwards and some to face outwards.

4 ✳ Using the clock face as a guide, place the waratah at 6 o'clock, the flannel flowers at 3 o'clock and 10 o'clock, and the Christmas bells at 12 and 7 o'clock.

5 ✳ Lastly, fill in with the small sprays of kurrajong, pink and brown boronia and Christmas bush. Any spaces that are too small to be filled with these can be filled with tiny holly leaves.

6 ✳ Make the card by rolling out the paste 5 cm (2 in) long by 2 cm (¾ in) wide. Neaten the edges and fold in half. Pack the inside of the card with some waxpaper to allow it to dry in an open position. When dry, pipe or write the greeting on the front. Attach with a small ribbon.

7 ✳ Place a bow made up of 3 colours at the back of the wreath and trail the ends either side of the wreath.

8 ✳ The side of the cake has a shell at the base with a row of piped lace just above this and green ribbon around the top edge.

Designs

Petals

Leaves

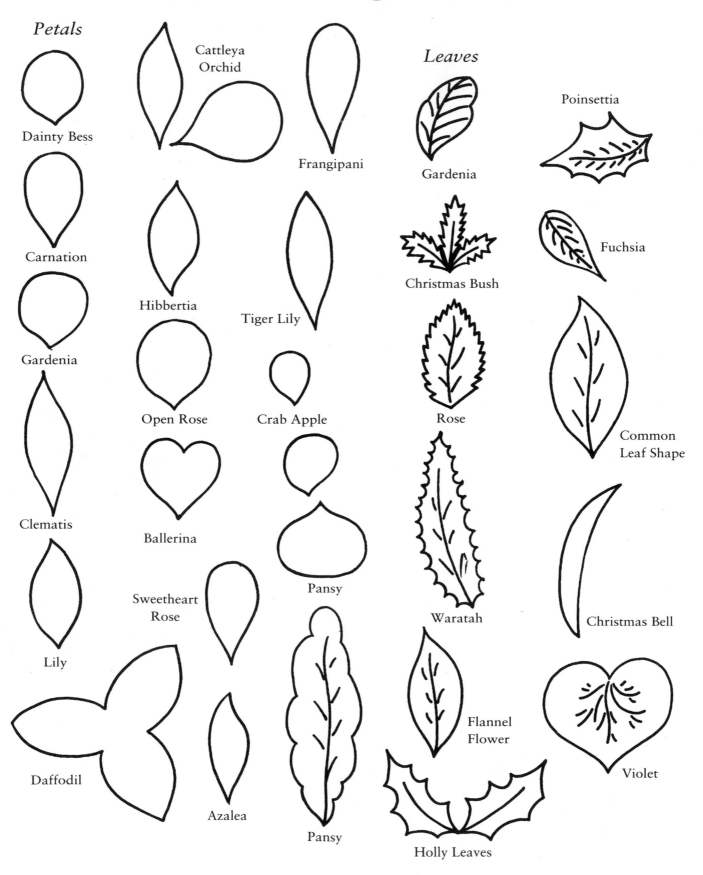

Dainty Bess

Cattleya Orchid

Frangipani

Gardenia

Poinsettia

Carnation

Hibbertia

Tiger Lily

Christmas Bush

Fuchsia

Gardenia

Open Rose

Crab Apple

Rose

Clematis

Ballerina

Common Leaf Shape

Lily

Sweetheart Rose

Pansy

Waratah

Christmas Bell

Daffodil

Azalea

Pansy

Flannel Flower

Holly Leaves

Violet

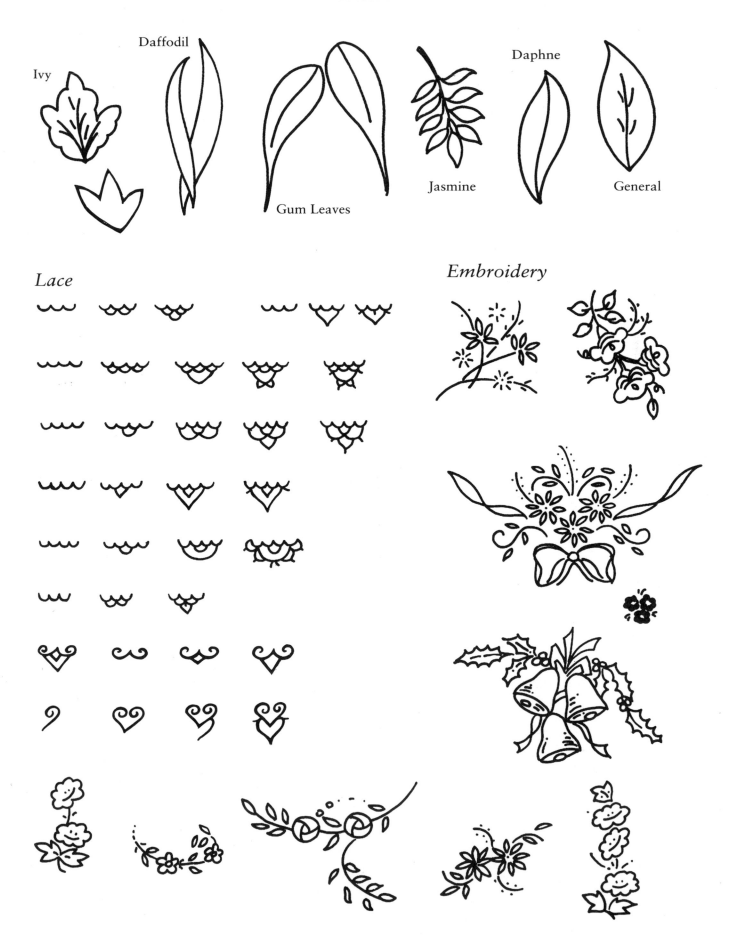

Ivy

Daffodil

Gum Leaves

Jasmine

Daphne

General

Lace

Embroidery

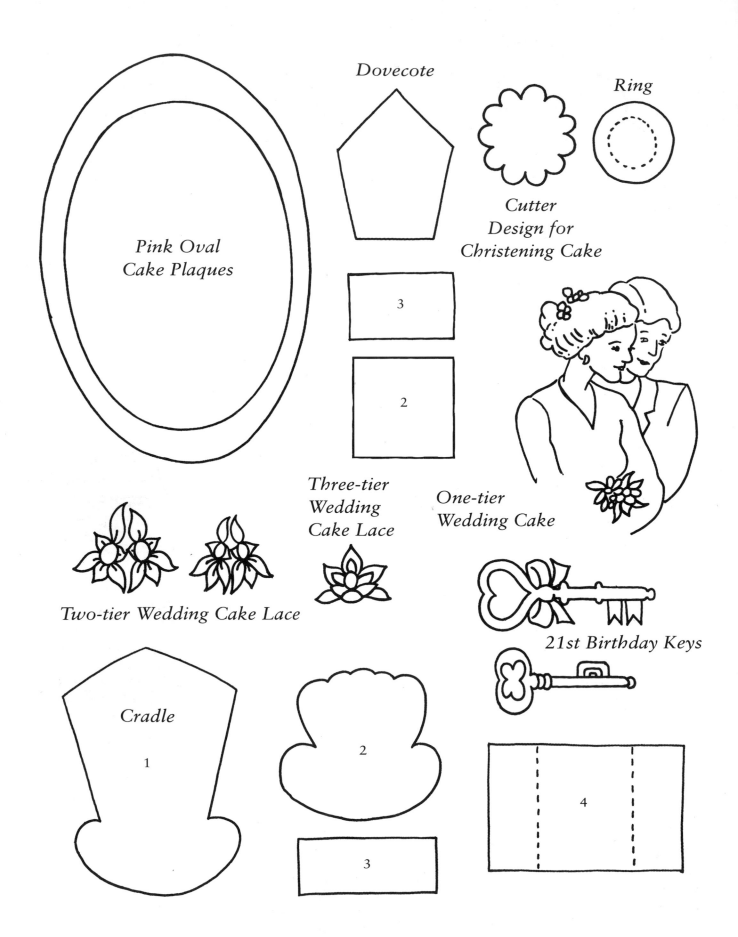

Dovecote

Ring

Pink Oval
Cake Plaques

Cutter
Design for
Christening Cake

3

2

Three-tier
Wedding
Cake Lace

One-tier
Wedding Cake

Two-tier Wedding Cake Lace

21st Birthday Keys

Cradle

1

2

3

4

Bibs

Christmas Cracker

Bible

Boy's
Christening
Cake

Pink Oval
Birthday Cake

Sole

Toe

Heel

Moulded Bootee

Knitted Bootee

Index